A COUNTRY DOCTOR'S *Journal*

Amazing Stories from Incredible Situations

Roger A. MacDonald, M.D.

Adventure Publications, Inc.
Cambridge, MN

D1410229

Dedication

This collection of stories is dedicated to:
Manley Elroy MacDonald,
a man of uncommon integrity.
And to
Mary Ellen (Porterfield) MacDonald
A woman of cheer and love.
These were my parents.

Cover and book design by Jonathan Norberg

10 9 8 7 6 5 4 3 2 1

Copyright 2007 by Dr. Roger A. MacDonald, M.D.
Published by Adventure Publications, Inc.
820 Cleveland St. S
Cambridge, MN 55008
1-800-678-7006
www.adventurepublications.net
Printed in U.S.A.
ISBN-13: 978-1-59193-210-9
ISBN-10: 1-59193-210-6

Table of Contents

Foreword by Dr. Joseph P. Connolly, M.D. 5

Introduction 7

I Dipped My Hands into the Stars 10

Medical School! 11

Surgery 14

Let Me Go 18

Bad Doc, Good Doc 20

Sirens in the Night 21

House Calls on the Brineless Briny 26

Consultants 29

A Frozen Section 30

The Importance of a Pathology Report 31

To Hitch a Ride 32

To Save a Soul 33

My Fellow Americans 36

A Wink and a Grin 40

The Staff of Life 43

Endless Love 44

Maple Nut Ice Cream 44

Randolph Zimmer 47

Frieda Schultz 52

Clinton 53

Until Death Do Us Part 55

Potpourri 58

I'm Sorry to Inform You 70

When To Have the Baby 74

Sulo 75

Is That You, Doc? 76

There Must Be an Alternative! 78

Office Humor 80

Special Delivery 81

Don't Ask 83

Rex Green 86

A Quiet Day Along Mistletoe Creek 91

We Know Ourselves 96
Critical Cosmetics 97
Isolation 98
Mort 100
A Joy of Family Practice 103
When You Least Expect It 104
Down a Dark Tunnel, Spinning 106
Viola 113
The Challenge of Obstetrics 116
The Message Heard 117
Alex 119
Cause and Effect 121
Swedish Ingenuity 123
Mirabel 125
A Fitting Memorial 128
A Signal Honor 130
Faith is a Wondrous Thing 131
Long Distance Medicine 133
Special Nurse 133
A Trip to the Hospital 134
Alternative Medicine 136
A Complication of Surgery 137
Miss Coughlin 140
And Finally 141
My Second-Most Unfavorite Job in the Whole World 143
Dr. Jack's House Call 145
Priorities 147
Stopwatch Medicine 149
The Stache 155
A Pearl is a Thing of Beauty 158
A New Sideline 160
A Date at the Cemetery 163
Black Rock Baby 165
Jan Torkelson 169
So, You Want to Be a Doctor 173

Foreword

The stories in this collection are true. They present glimpses into real-life physician-patient encounters, gleaned from Dr. MacDonald's forty-six years of rural medical experience. In addition, he contacted many of his Minnesota colleagues and asked them to share their recollections of the joys and adventures of being "front-line physicians."

Today, barriers of bureaucracy and "busy-ness" have risen between doctor and patient. A casualty can be a sense of common humanity. Physicians become "Providers" instead of "Doc," while a patient so easily evolves into some roadblock to keeping an efficient schedule. Medicine is becoming "Production" oriented. These stories return the heart of medicine to where it belongs, the physician using knowledge and skill to help his or her patient.

Ensuring adequate services in out-state settings is a complex challenge. For much of rural Minnesota (and our state is not alone in this), medical care depends on broadly-trained doctors: family physicians, general internists, full-range pediatricians and general surgeons.

How to ensure a supply of such doctors was recognized as a challenge by administrators at two campuses of the University of Minnesota Medical School System. From its inception, the medical school at the University of Minnesota-Duluth accepted as a founding principle the training of students for a rural practice. Beginning in 1970, leaders at the Minneapolis campus of the University of Minnesota Medical School also adopted the goal of providing increased numbers of physicians for rural areas of our state. A unique and aptly named academic effort began. Termed the Rural Physician Associate Program or, affectionately, R-PAP, its thrust was to encourage a student to enter a rural practice. It was conceived by Dr. John Verby, M.D. Volunteer third-year medical students were placed in rural health care facilities for nine to twelve months as part of their formal training. They received close, hour by hour teaching and supervision from qualified frontline physicians. Students learned first-hand that a quality life and competent medical care were possible beyond the city limits of a large urban area.

By now, approximately 1,100 students have taken part in this program. Its example has encouraged similar efforts at medical schools across the nation. In addition to being a grand way to learn clinical medicine, it has succeeded in its goal of persuading graduates to practice where they are most needed.

Through efforts of our universities, through programs such as R-PAP, through the wonderful legacy of former learners teaching new learners, this unique method of teaching can continue for years to come. It is a bond assuring compassionate care of fellow citizens.

Our friends!

Dr. Joseph P. Connolly, M.D.
Emeritus Associate Professor
Co-Director R-PAP (1970–1975)
Department of Family Medicine and
  Community Health
Medical School, University of Minnesota
Minneapolis, Minnesota

Introduction

What exactly is a country doctor? More than someone who lives outside big-city limits? A mythic figure to quell fear when it rides the land? An embodiment of strength and wisdom? A person, above all. Ready at hand, compassionate when callous nature strikes. A companion who knows the way to one's home. One whose black satchel carries healing and hope.

A friend.

Those colleagues whom I regard most warmly are fellow country doctors. Similar challenges forge bonds. The endless necessity to keep up on medical advances. The strain of endless emergency call. The endless anxieties that go with practicing in a remote area, where a person with devastating injury or illness can arrive in the office or emergency room. The endless tasks of balancing family responsibilities with demands of medicine!

That rural America needs improved access to health care is evident. Recognition of the fact underlies the recent formation of a division within the Minnesota Department of Health, The Office of Rural Health and Primary Care.

I have heard history described as being of two main streams: top-down or bottom-up. If one considers top-down history as being textbook material, presidents and wars and epochal events, then one can view bottom-up history as events seen through the eyes of an individual. In a diary, a memoir. This collection of stories, of memories, is of the latter variety. It has its own claim to validity; the stories reflect real incidents from ordinary lives.

Still, is any life ordinary?

Confidentiality is a keystone to a professional relationship. How, then, to share the courage, resourcefulness, the humor(!) of my patients within such constrictions was an ever-present challenge. To alter names was obvious, but in a small community not always enough. I changed the locations of my practice towns, dubbing them Northpine. (It is on no map.) When possible, I secured permission from the patient/friend involved to use his or her story. I smudged non-essential details in order to preserve the heart of a person's experience. I pray that I offend no one and that others can learn from the joys and fortitude of my neighbors.

That health care sails troubled seas these days is front-page news. Need exceeds availability. A specter of financial disaster caused by unexpected illness looms over all but the most affluent. We are increasingly locked into a delivery system based on tiers, those with insurance . . . comprehensive care . . . and those without, where yawning flaws in the system can prevent a person's receiving even minimal attention. The profession of medicine squirms on the dilemma of whether it provides a service (guaranteeing access for all) or is primarily a business (with profit the decision-maker). Is it not obvious that pharmacy flounders in a similar quagmire of crossed purpose?

I consider myself fortunate. At mid-twentieth century, when my practice years began, such questions barely rumbled on a far horizon.

A small-town practice is so personal. Patients become friends, and friends become patients. One earns esteem; it is not conferred by small print on a diploma.

The life I led as a rural physician was not unique. A number of friends, other country doctors, have submitted accounts of events from their own practices to be herein included. I am grateful to these colleagues for sharing of the wealth from their lives.

The following friends and colleagues have contributed stories to this journal:

Dr. Kenneth Carter, M.D.
Dr. Joseph P. Connolly, M.D.
Dr. Norman Hagberg, M.D.
Dr. "Jack", M.D.
Dr. C. Paul Martin, M.D.
Dr. Michael McCarthy, M.D.
Dr. Robert P. Meyer, M.D.
Dr. Robert Nelson, M.D.
Dr. Robert H. Nelson, M.D.

Dr. Vern Olmanson, M.D.
Dr. Ricard Puumala, M.D.
Dr. Thomas Stolee, M.D.
Dr. John Watkins, M.D.

Unless otherwise indicated, opinions expressed within these pages are those of the author.

Time treats past events indifferently when memory becomes less than dust. We whose stories are here included offer tribute to some of our old friends, in hopes they will be remembered a while longer.

—Roger A. MacDonald, M.D.

Roger A. MacDonald, M.D., served as a family physician in rural Minnesota from 1948 to 1980, when he was appointed associate director of the Rural Physician Associate Program at the University of Minnesota Medical School. Currently retired, Dr. MacDonald resides in Grand Marais, Minnesota, and La Verne, California.

I Dipped My Hands into the Stars

In the Boundary Waters, between Canada and the USA,
  The holy dwells.
  All earthly beauty is reflected in the mirror of fresh water:
    Tall green pines rooted deeply against the storms,
    Large gray rocks etched with ancient life,
    Shrubs of tiny blueberries, delicious in morning pancakes,
    And the bluest of blue skies.

All is silence.
  There are no motor boats, no cars, not even airplanes.
  No harsh sounds to break the quiet.
  Only the soft sounds of nature:
    The lap of water gently kissing the rocky shores,
    A cool breeze playing in the pines,
    And the occasional haunting cry of the loon.
With no calendar to keep,
Each moment is awake,
  Alert to life
  And her beauty.

  One night I stumbled through the dark
    looking for a place to rinse my hands.
  Having camped on a small island in this watery world,
    I could find the lake in any direction ahead.
  When I found a dark patch of water
    I looked out across the lake's great expanse.
  The distant trees etched black shapes against the starry sky.
    For a moment, I just stood in awe.

  Then I knelt to wash my hands.
  My eyes focused on the stars scattered before me.
    The watery mirror brought them right to my feet!
    I caught my breath.
  It was a holy moment
    When I dipped my hands into the stars.

But we all live
  in Boundary Waters,
    Where the holy fills the mundane.
When I run water to wash my dishes,
  Am I aware
  that once again
    I dip my hands into the stars?

Kathryn Pfaltzgraff

Medical School!

*There is no avoiding it. To become a doctor, one must
attend medical school. That idea is astonishingly recent. For
most of human history, a physician (healer, priest, barber,
incantator, magician, muskekewinini . . . medicine man, in
the lexicon of my Ojibwe in-laws) learned his or her craft as
an apprentice to someone already established. The modern
idea of Science put a lasting crimp in that approach.*

I recently attended the sixtieth anniversary of graduating
from the University of Minnesota Medical School in
Minneapolis, Minnesota. Classmates, so many have fallen.
Nostalgia was rampant when we summoned the ghosts of
shared memories. *The rigors of lecture and clinical training.
Midnight study sessions and endless tests. Most unforgettable
professors. Ah . . .*

The faculty of a medical school includes a lively collection
of geniuses. Eccentricity flourishes. A comrade and I vied
to recall the most memorable personality from a panoply
of candidates. Super-erudite-and-proud-of-it Doctor . . .
discretion suggests leaving some names to history, where they
quietly reside. The anatomy prof whose oft-voiced ambition
upon his death was to have his various parts preserved in jars
of formaldehyde, thus allowing him to "teach" far beyond the
constrictions of a lifetime? The instructor whose middle initial
"P" surely stood for Pomposity? The surgeon whose secondary
aim in life seemed to be the shriveling of medical students over
irritation at having to squander research time teaching them?
Wait . . .

Call him Doctor Genius, for he came rightly by such
a name. He taught neural anatomy. The man's physique
was a slender but muscled question mark. Gray hair obeyed
no comb. Lines in lean cheeks enclosed a wide mouth in
parentheses. An oversized jaw suggested strength of character.
Humor had left telltale marks about his eyes. A long white

coat, the designated uniform of a university physician, partially concealed garb suggesting that of a cowboy at home on the range. I have forgotten the style of his footwear. Boots? He was genial, kindly and a devoted teacher. He told us one day that he had grown up on a ranch in Montana. Finances were ever precarious. He had an identical twin brother. When the issue of education arose during a family council, it was decided that one lad should attend college, while the other stayed on at the ranch. As he told it, "We flipped a coin to see which brother did what. I lost and had to leave the ranch for school."

A steeply-tiered anatomy department amphitheatre served as arena for his classes. He bounced across the floor below our high ranging seats like a hyperactive cricket. He raised ambidexterity to mystifying heights. Using chalks of a dozen hues, he rapidly and accurately sketched neural pathways of the human brain on broad blackboards at the front of the room. With both hands. At the same time! All the while, over his shoulder, he kept up a staccato explanation of what he was illustrating.

We students were enthralled.

One day he lowered a second blackboard in front of a maze of brilliant drawings on the stationary board. Dangling from a pair of wires, it promptly reacted to Dr. Genius' scribbling and began to sway side to side, faster and faster. The good doctor side-stepped with its motion, back and forth, never missing a color or line. His audience began to titter. To keep up with his blackboard, he trotted faster.

A backhanded swipe knocked the spectacles from his face. Dr. Genius seemed unaware. Our sniggers grew up. Then, in his trotting back and forth (still sketching rapidly), he trampled the glasses and reduced them to rubble. We students strangled. Oblivious to what lay underfoot, he completed his diagram and returned to a podium. Without a hitch, he reached into a pocket and brought out another pair of glasses, which he hooked in place.

We exploded, drowning out the man's earnest explanation of his drawings. When the laughter had subsided to a low rumble, he paused suddenly, peered over glasses-number-two at us and said, "Don't worry about those others; I'll grind them down and make a little-bitty pair." We applauded lustily, while Doctor Genius stared at us in bewilderment.

Dr. Rasmussen—there! I revealed your name!—the intricacy of your drawings made the human nervous system less daunting to understand, but what comes to me through the filter of time is your gift of humanity, with its gentle quirks.

Belatedly, thank you!

Surgery

Few branches of medicine command the mystique that the public accords surgery. To violate anatomy, rearrange body parts and remove diseased organs creates the deepest awe among those outside the profession. Awe is appropriate. Still, to risk disillusionment, might I suggest that surgeons are actually people?

Some of my best friends are surgeons. Not that I'd want my daughter to marry one, you understand.

Prestige and remuneration favor him or her who wields a scalpel. Still, in no way do I envy my surgical colleagues. He (and with increasing frequency, she) spent many extra years in training. He works hard physically. She has a high rate of varicose veins in her legs, all those hours of standing stock-still. He tends toward a stoop-shouldered physique, probably from all those same hours of leaning to peer into a surgical wound. She is a prime target of litigious patients and their attorneys. He tends to have a high IQ, not all bad, of course. A pecking order is well developed. Subtle, but snappish. Most are good parents and loving spouses. I'm under the impression quite a few attend church. He is grand company, a raconteur of the highest skill. I've known surgeons who were humble, genial, kind, unafraid of tackling new challenges beyond the comfort of established activities.

Given these verities, I am left to wonder at the exceptions. A personality like a grizzly bear with a toothache? Let me tell you about Dr. Growly and Dr. Howler.*

Because of the jet-propelled educational pace mandated by World War II, I was twenty-two years old the day I began my internship at St. Lukes Hospital in Duluth, Minnesota. My father always proclaimed, "We MacDonalds are late bloomers." For me, that translated into trepidation at the responsibility I was about to assume as The Doctor.

*Names changed to protect the guilty.

One of my first month-long hospital training rotations was surgery.

Dr. Growly, sixtyish, was from the old school. Finesse is for sissies, empathy (whatever the hell that is) for those too timid to do a man's work. His basic philosophy was, "See it, whack it out."

We interns were expected to bring proficiency in tying ligatures to the operating table. Unfortunately, proficiency requires more than a few nights spent in the interns' quarters tying knots in thread fastened to the back of a chair. Add the angst of an information force-fed, genuine late-bloomer . . .

Dr. Growly placed a series of sutures and waited expectantly for me to tie knots in them. I tied one, slowly and carefully. Probably the tip of my tongue stuck out. Concentration. Hard to tell behind a surgical mask.

"Goddam, Doctor," he growled. "We don't have all day. Speed it up."

"Yessir."

I put speed—call it heft—into the next tie, and the suture broke.

"God," Dr. Growly said. Maybe not with reverence.

He replaced the broken suture. I tied it, more . . . carefully.

Dr. Growly jiggled in place, glared at the wall clock. I took the loose ends of another suture and cinched it up.

It broke.

"God-*damn*." Genuine feeling. Unrestrained.

Sweat dripped off my eyelids into the smothering mask covering my face. My glasses steamed up. I waited while he replaced the ligature. My fingers had developed what doctors call an intention tremor. I broke the suture.

"Doctor, you aren't tying up the *Queen Mary*!"

"Yessir. No sir. Quite, sir."

My rubber surgical gloves were filling with sweat. Squishy.

Maggie was the nurse-anesthetist on the case, a "seen-it-all" veteran. She scribbled on a sheet of paper and held up her message.

Tell him to go to hell.

I didn't, but looking back, I kind of wish I had.

———————

Dr. Howler's tirades were renowned, even among
the storied ranks of cranky surgeons. An alpha screamer.
Operating room ethics include permission for The Surgeon
to blame someone else for Any Little Mishap (ALM), say, a
bleeder requiring a second ligature to control it. An intern is
convenient to assign responsible for ALM, is captive and still
well down the hierarchical totem pole. Not in the best position
to fire back. An alternative ploy to cope with ALM is to throw
a surgical instrument. The clatter of a hemostat or large wound
retractor when it strikes the wall soothes marvelously.

Still, most authorities agree that there is no better target
for righteous spleen than a nurse. Typically, two nurses attend
the doctors performing an operation. A scrub nurse wears a
sterilized surgical gown, gloves and a mask, the same as the
physicians. She stands alongside them, doling out surgical
instruments and supplies as needed. She (and increasingly, he)
is the "scrub" nurse. A second nurse, wearing operating-room
garb but no gloves or sterile gown, "circulates" about the room.
She opens supplies or instruments as needed, transferring them
to her colleague with a pair of sterilized tongs.

One day I sat at the transcription desk in the surgical suite,
doing my internly job of recording what had been performed
during a freshly completed operation.

A bellow rattled the door to Operating Room Two. My
pen skittered across the desk, and I trotted along the hall to
peer through a viewing window.

Annie McGinty was the circulating nurse that day. I
observed what happened next. Dr. Howler held a pair of
dampened, 10-by-12-inch operative cloths, what are called
laparotomy sponges, or "laps" for short. His squinty little eyes
glared at Annie over the top of his mask.

"I want *hot laps*," he roared.

Annie mumbled, "Sorry." She opened a new package
of laps and handed them to the scrub nurse, who hurriedly
dipped them in a basin of warm, sterile water before passing

them on to Dr. Howler.

The man massaged them with gloved hands, his eyebrows cocked in contemplation. He fired a fastball at the far wall, a gob of wet laps. Splat.

"I want *hot laps!*" he screeched.

Now, our Miss Annie's auburn hair bore honest testimony to her temperament. Her forehead above the white gauze covering the lower part of her face assumed the glow of a gorgeous sunset. She seized a sterile metal pitcher, strode to the hot water tap set into one wall, filled it with visibly steaming water, tromped back to the basin beside her colleague, and poured it full to the brim. Next, she retrieved her sterile tongs, snatched a pair of laps off the back table, plunged them into the cauldron of simmering water, and dropped them into Dr. Howler's hands.

"Here," Annie snarled, "catch them before they cool off."

His eyes popped and he juggled them like—well, like really hot laps.

It would be uplifting to report that such spirit had been rewarded. In fact, Annie was fired. God must not be challenged so blatantly in his own domain.

Let Me Go

I regarded my relationship with a patient as a contract between partners. I provided training and experience; the patient was entitled to know what was happening and had a right to help make decisions. Sounds simple, but with implications.

I had just moved to the community on Lake Superior's North Shore where I still live. I first encountered Josephine in the aisles of Johnson's Food Market. She struggled to separate one package of laundry soap from its fellows while at the same time juggling a cane, both with her right hand. I realized that her left arm was shriveled, held tight against her side in the manner of one riven by a stroke. When she thanked me for handing the box into her cart, I saw that one eye was locked uselessly to the side. Her speech was intelligible, but with a hitch, a hesitancy.

Josephine consulted me in my new office a few months later. I have forgotten the reason for her visit. She was fifty-something at the time, plump, pleasant and clear mentally. I asked about her neurological problems.

"I was twenty-two," she said. "It was during labor when I was having my daughter. They told me a blood vessel burst in my head. I've been the same ever since." She looked down for a moment, then straight at me. "Since that has come up, Doctor, I have a request. If I ever have a bad stroke, one like you read about where you are unconscious and aren't going to get any better—I don't want to be kept alive with feeding tubes and—that kind of thing. If it happens, and you are my doctor, would you just let me go?"

Let me go.

I heard those same three words many times over the years. My mother-in-law mumbled them to my wife, Barbara, and me during the one lucid moment she had while enduring those degrading last days of her life. And I remember the dear friend dying of lung cancer who, when I awakened her during hospital rounds each morning, blinked at me, then said, "Oh no, I'm still here. Let me go."

Josephine and I made a pact: No therapeutic heroics, no prolongation of a vegetative condition. No feeding tubes. We did not sign any papers, and no one thought to involve an attorney. Our pact was in words and understanding and belief in each other. That philosophy left over from generations past, that "My handshake is my bond," sealed our agreement.

Years went their way. I received a call from the hospital one evening. Ambulance arrived. Patient unconscious. Need you.

The patient's breathing was stertorous, her body flaccid, and she made no response to even painful stimuli. Characteristic neurological signs indicated massive brain damage. Josephine had suffered the "wipe-out" stroke she had dreaded. Now decisions were on my shoulders by way of our pact.

I conferred with a daughter and grandchildren, informed them of our agreement those years before.

"She told us," they said.

Times change, social pressures alter. Politicians involve themselves and guarantees between two people can be called into question.

I squared my shoulders, figuratively.

"I intend to honor our pact," I told the family. Her daughter nodded quietly. I said, "I will give her intravenous salt solution and water, because dehydration is hideous for all of us."

"As you decide," her daughter said.

I made daily hospital rounds on Josephine. She never stirred; her coma never lightened. And she survived without an ounce of nutrition for twenty-seven days. My resolve was a battered husk by the end of that time. Memory of the pleading in her eye, come down through those intervening years, sustained me, and I am sure that I did what she wanted.

My pact with Josephine was not unique. I know from conversations with colleagues that, "Let me go," is still quietly honored.

DR. ROBERT H. NELSON, M.D., CONTRIBUTED THE NEXT TWO STORIES

Dr. Robert H. Nelson, M.D., is a Family Physician. He practiced for twenty-two years in Hastings, Minnesota, before joining the staff of the Mayo Clinic in Rochester, where he currently works with a research team studying type two diabetes. Let me introduce you to Dr. Nelson, using his own words as he describes incidents from his practice:

Bad Doc, Good Doc

Many of the decisions made by a doctor impact a patient's daily life. Having to advise an elderly person to cease driving an automobile qualifies. Most people resent losing driving privileges. Agnes was such a person. She was in early stages of Alzheimer's disease, but still able to live alone with the assistance of family members.

One day a sister escorted Agnes to my office. Agnes was cheerful but had no idea why she had been brought to see me. Her sister took me aside and told me that several days earlier, Agnes had driven to the grocery store and become lost on her way home. Fortunately, she had found her sister's home before any tragedies occurred. Her sister did not want her to drive anymore, but lacked the courage to tell her so. She asked if I would do it for her.

As I conversed with Agnes, it was evident that her dementia was progressing. Tragically, Alzheimer's assaults not only memory. Poor judgment, loss of abstract thinking, inability to problem-solve, even to perform tasks of daily living result. It can rob people of social inhibitions. Agnes, sweet and proper, even prim, hovered on the brink of disintegration of her personality.

I asked Agnes about her trip to the grocery. She had only vague recollections of the event and downplayed its significance. I explained to her that this episode was a sign of disease progression. I told her she could no longer drive a car. She erupted into a tirade, using language that a hack Hollywood writer would hesitate to use. She accused me of greed, incompetence and lack of caring. Her sister huddled into the corner of her chair in an agony of embarrassment. Agnes threatened to kill herself if I "took away her license." Her death would be my fault.

Eventually I calmed her enough that she was no longer shouting, but her voice and glare bore icicles when she stomped from my office.

Six weeks later, I again found Agnes's name on my appointment schedule. I approached the exam-room door with apprehension. I put on what I hoped was my most disarming smile and walked into the room. Agnes greeted me cordially. She was in a chatty mood and skipped through a series of topics.

Eventually, I steered the conversation to how she was coping now that she no longer had a car. She brushed my attempt aside as though it was an inconsequential matter. As the visit terminated, she squeezed my hand between both of hers and smiled broadly.

"Thank you, Doctor. You're such a nice man, not at all like that other guy. He wouldn't let me drive!"

Sirens in the Night

It seems so long ago that I sat in an auditorium, waiting to receive the diploma decreeing that I had become a medical doctor. There was one more lecture to hear, that called the commencement address. I do not recall the name of the physician-poet who delivered it, but I haven't forgotten its message. He spoke eloquently of the life changes that happen when one becomes a doctor. Never again, he said, would we experience the world in quite the same way. Daily events would take on new meaning. The example, upon which he built his talk, was the sound of a siren in the night. How true his words were! To this day, I cannot hear a siren in the distance and darkness without feeling a knot in my stomach. What does the sound foretell? Someone gravely injured, fighting for life? Some other catastrophe in a person's life? Even, a false alarm?

I recalled those words and thoughts recently when I happened across a popular prime-time television program known for its use of gruesome imagery. I could not watch. Events on the screen were too close to those in an emergency room. The next day, as I took a stroll around my neighborhood, I was moved to reflect on some of the more dramatic moments of my career. Some were brief. In most cases, I do not recall names. Yet, they etched indelible marks on my memory, on who I am as a physician. As a person.

Call him Charlie. He was a fifteen-month-old toddler who had only recently learned to take his first faltering steps. I never saw him alive. I had to piece together details of the accident that had claimed him.

His father was backing a car out of the garage so he could take his young family on a picnic. Charlie's mother was packing food. Each had assumed the other was keeping an eye on their only son.

When I arrived at the emergency room, I found the staff working on the boy with every tool at their disposal. A tube had been inserted into his windpipe to allow the anesthetist to breathe for him. Another had been inserted into his stomach to remove any air that might have been blown down his esophagus. An intravenous line had been inserted into each arm. Fluids poured into him to raise blood pressure. An intern expertly administered cardiopulmonary resuscitation (CPR). The emergency room chief resident studied the latest lab results and a cardiogram.

Somehow, in the rush to perform all the duties they had been trained to do, nobody seemed actually to have stepped back to look at Charlie. His head was terribly misshapen. A gray mushy substance oozed from his right ear. Brain substance! In effect, the ER staff was earnestly trying to resuscitate a corpse.

As the attending physician in charge of the case, it fell onto my shoulders to call an end to attempts at revival. My next duty was to go to the small private room where terrified family members waited and inform Charlie's parents that the boy was dead. I did my best to give them something that was not mine to give, consolation.

Charlie's father stared blankly ahead, hearing little or nothing when I introduced myself. Over and over he repeated, "I didn't know he was there. I didn't know . . ."

Charlie's mother watched my face tearfully, obviously searching for any sign of good news. As gently as I could, I told them. I sat for a while in a vain attempt to comfort—until I was summoned for another case.

Another case.

Is it possible to become "case-hardened?"

If it were so, a protective shield, a Teflon-like coat to let a doctor go home and sleep of a night, where is it to be found? The scent of newly-shed blood, the sweat of anguished personnel who must watch a life seep away, grief's nearly palpable aura: why do the miasmas of any emergency room not stay chastely confined within hospital walls?

Mr. Olson was driving through our community when he passed out and slammed his car into a telephone pole. When I arrived in the emergency room, the ER physician had stabilized him as best he could, but the man's heart rate remained ominously fast and his blood pressure was unacceptably low.

Staff members and I quickly reviewed the extent of his known injuries and those treatments begun. Everything seemed to have been done correctly, yet Mr. Olson had not responded to the efforts. Clearly, we were missing something. Then, I was hit by an idea. We had assumed that the high pulse rate and low blood pressure had been caused by the accident. What if the reverse was true?

Injuries cause shock, characterized by low blood pressure.

23

Reflexes try to correct the situation by delivering more blood to circulation via a speeded-up pulse. What if the accident had been caused by a medical condition we call tachycardia, a rapid heart rate that causes the blood pressure to fall? I reviewed his electrocardiogram (EKG) and saw that my new diagnosis was plausible. I called for appropriate treatment, in this case a low level electrical shock to the chest to interrupt the aberrant impulses dominating his heart.

His heart slowed immediately to a normal rate, and his blood pressure returned to normal. We had done it, a life saved.

I transferred Mr. Olson to the intensive care unit (ICU). I talked with the ER staff for a few minutes, then went to the ICU to finish an admitting examination and to write orders.

Mr. Olson's blood pressure had again fallen. Once more, it seemed that we were missing something. I realized that his abdomen had swollen until it resembled that of a woman eight months pregnant. This finding had appeared since leaving the emergency room and could mean only one thing. Mr. Olson had received internal injuries and was either bleeding into his abdomen, or he was filling up with air from a ruptured intestine.

I summoned our community surgeon. He arrived within minutes and agreed with my diagnosis. Since this was in the days prior to high-tech, noninvasive tests such as CT scans and MRI, we prepared for exploratory surgery.

Thirty minutes later, we were in the operating room, ready to begin. Transfusions had restored normal blood pressure, and we felt confident that we could save him.

Within minutes, our confidence was shattered. As soon as we opened his belly, we saw that there was not a localized, single injury. Blood oozed from all directions. A quick look at the liver revealed the reason.

Mr. Olson had advanced cirrhosis of the liver. A cirrhotic liver cannot make essential blood-clotting factors. We knew we could transfuse necessary clotting factors and keep him alive if we could just identify a main source of blood loss and stop the bleeding. What we could not do was pour in enough clotting factors to stop the generalized oozing from every surface in view. Nevertheless, we tried. Fresh-frozen plasma. Platelet transfusions.

We were losing.

After a length of time that seemed like hours, even days, the surgeon and I looked at each other and nodded. It was time to stop. We bowed our heads and watched Mr. Olson die.

These are representative of the memories that flashed through my mind while I took that walk. I recalled each with such a sense of sadness. I also knew that my commencement-day poet had been right. I was changed. For me, violence, brutality, suffering and death became too much a part of real life. They could never be a source of prime time entertainment.

• • •

House Calls on the Brineless Briny

The terms "house call" and "country doctor" do so readily join hands.

"Did you really make house calls?"

Such a revealing question. To those rural physicians from my vintage, the answer is, "Of course." Clearly, the high tech medicine of today cannot be carried to someone's home in a little black bag. Still, the number of queries I receive, and their wistful tone, suggests that the public—our patients—feels that something is missing from what medicine offers today. What if it is something important?

Sometimes, "house call" needs to be defined more precisely.

The northeastern corner of Minnesota forms one hundred and fifty miles of mighty Lake Superior's northern shoreline. The lake was first named by Europeans because of its "superior" elevation above sea level, compared to the four other Great Lakes. We who are fortunate enough to live beside it appreciate its superiority in broader scale. Its face can shine, Gitchee Gammi, for those who pause to see. Its blue can challenge the most azure of skies. Its moods are painted large on nature's canvas; they vary by season and time of day. Fog dense as grey cotton muffles any view of reefs capable of sinking a second Titanic. On a morning when air temperatures are twenty or thirty below zero, wisps of frozen mist rise from its surface to crowd together crookedly, mirroring smoke from chimneys on land. Waves so seldom silent sweep gravel onto shore, to the sound of a thousand gentle castanets, only to reclaim loaned pebbles with the next wave in line. Sometimes ice shackles the restless water, and Superior becomes a version of the arctic.

The lake struggles to shrug off man's casual pollution. Yet, it rewards us with sparkles and smiles even in its pain. When aroused by November's passion, it dashes tsunamis against the rocky headlands containing it. Hundreds of boats, great and small, lie buried in its dark, icy depths. Superior must never be taken for granted!

Its vital statistics are impressive: broadest body of fresh water on earth; the third largest volume of contained fresh water among the world's grandest lakes. Its greatest depth is more than thirteen hundred feet.

I have made "home visits" aboard three separate ore carriers on Lake Superior. For those who do not know, iron ore and taconite iron pellets are hauled in enormously long boats that load cargo at Minnesota ports in Taconite Harbor, Silver Bay, Two Harbors and Duluth. These products of Minnesota's famed Mesabi Iron Range mines end up in places like Youngstown, Ohio, and Pittsburgh, Pennsylvania. Driblets return to the north country in the form of our latest-model sedans. The boats range in length from six or eight hundred feet to more than a thousand. That's a fifth of a mile, to give you perspective. From the dock alongside, a boat's steel bulwarks, painted black or barn-red, tower overhead. A hatch near the bow opens onto internal catwalks stretching toward the rear, alongside bins holding pellets. Cacophony and dust, light bulbs that tickle darkness without dispelling it. Quarters for the crew are at the very aft of the boat, prison-sparse cells.

One of my calls aboard such a boat was to treat a seaman who was a foreign national. Immigration authorities would not let him come ashore at Taconite Harbor, because the place he called home was on some taboo list. What lurking menace he posed I did not understand, but I recall thinking that he seemed like an ordinary guy, if with an accent. Makes a person wonder how ultimately ferocious are all of those "others" we "have been lovingly taught to hate and fear," in the poignant words of Rodgers and Hammerstein.

On a second occasion, a sailor thoughtlessly had a heart attack just after an ore carrier had cleared its loading dock and headed down-lake. Time is money with these symbols of corporate America, and the captain was not about to return to dockside so the guy could easily be taken ashore.

As is usual with so many house calls, the request came

after midnight (Murphy's Law number twenty-eight, I believe). The boat arrived at 3 a.m., stopping just outside the breakwater guarding Grand Marais' harbor. I was summoned to the Coast Guard Station, plopped still half asleep into one of those overgrown lifeboats the service uses, and was ferried out to the side of the ore carrier. Up close, those suckers are big! We . . . well, mostly I clung to any handhold . . . got the patient down from the deck in some kind of metal basket affair, secured him in the Coast Guard lifeboat, and we headed for shore. By the time we reached the dock, the ore carrier was already well out to sea. I've been told it takes the better part of a mile to stop one of those monsters when it is loaded with ore and has gained momentum, but can their great propellers churn out acceleration!

The patient healed, even sent me a Christmas card one year.

My third call aboard an ore carrier came about because of Lake Superior's love affair with November gales. When a boat is coming up-lake . . . that's us here in Minnesota . . . it pumps ballast while still a ways out from shore. (Ballast: filthy, cruddy water that has been known to catch on fire while still loose in Cleveland's Cuyahoga River—Ohio's attempt to clean up and recycle some of its worst effluent to Lake Superior. Of course, eventually it returns to Lake Erie. Fair enough.)

To enter Taconite Harbor's bay and shipping dock, the boat must do a turn just beforehand, a matter of ninety to more than one hundred degrees. For a while it is broadside to any little breeze out of the northeast. A real gale will set that lightened boat to rolling side to side, rivaling any ride in an amusement park. My patient that night (yes, three o'clock again) became hysterical, convinced the boat was going to capsize, not a totally unreasonable assumption. He refused to stay on board for a return trip down-lake. No one at the ore-loading facility was quite sure what to do with him, so they called me. I gave the man a sedative and a ride to the hospital in Grand Marais for what was left of the night.

The guy had a better night's rest than I did.

DR. TOM STOLEE, M.D., CONTRIBUTED THE NEXT FIVE STORIES

Doctor Tom Stolee, M.D., a fellow in the American College of Pathologists, is a decades-long friend and mentor. As he acknowledges, he had the good sense while in medical school in Minneapolis to marry the daughter of a Norwegian fisherman from Minnesota's North Shore. His own Norse forebears gave approval in unusually flowery language: "Good." Years of consultation in rural hospitals solidified for Dr. Stolee a respect for the role of a country doctor. In his words, "The most critical part of medicine is primary care. The country doc has the most difficult job in medicine." Further, "If anyone does not have access to affordable health care, then we have failed as a profession!" These values guided Dr. Stolee's career. During a stint as president of the Minnesota Medical Association, and as a delegate to the American Medical Association for more than a decade, he championed the cause of rural medicine. He was equally dedicated to improving the quality and availability of health care to minority people, both urban and in Minnesota's far-flung reservations. He lived what he preached and even in retirement continues to advocate for rural health issues.

Let me introduce Dr. Tom Stolee through a few stories from our common experiences:

Consultants

Medicine's broad panoply of knowledge expands like the shock wave of an explosion. Specialists . . . consultants . . . keep a patient healthy and a country doctor sane. Thank you, good colleagues.

Perhaps the most trying part of being the only doctor for miles in all directions was—being the only doctor for miles in all directions. No one with whom to commune. To state the obvious, medicine, the science and art, is complex. City colleagues have consultants down every corridor. During my years of frontline rural practice, I had in-office colleagues less than half of that time. There is no more lonely a feeling than to arrive at office or hospital emergency room and find some catastrophe for which my experience and training are sketchy at best. There is simply too much to know!

Over the years, two highly specialized kinds of doctors came willingly to visit my remote community, and on a regular basis: A radiologist and a pathologist.

Our visiting radiology consultant spent one day a week in town. He read every x-ray taken during the previous week, a safety net for patient and physician alike. I particularly remember and honor Gib and Fred for all they did for us.

Besides performing autopsies, a pathologist examines tissues removed during surgery. An ultimate diagnosis depends on what a microscope reveals. There is NO place for guesswork in medicine! The discipline of pathology also includes supervision of laboratory procedures, vital quality control. For years, we were thus blessed during twice-a-month visits from a Duluth pathologist. In addition, he provided timely updates on current concepts in medicine, essential to keeping up for an isolated doctor. Thank you, Art and Tom and Dave.

A Frozen Section

A visiting surgeon was due in our North Shore hospital one wintry Wednesday morning. I would assist him in removing a man's stone-filled gallbladder. A woman had consulted me the day before regarding a lump in one breast. She needed a biopsy to make sure that it was not cancer. Dr. Tom, our visiting pathologist, was also due on the same Wednesday morning. I worked the telephone. Dr. Tom, could you, would you do a frozen section of the lump if Dr. Surgeon would agree? Ever helpful, Dr. Tom agreed that he could bring

the equipment necessary to do the test. Next, I called Dr.
Surgeon; could you, would you, biopsy and if positive, do the
necessary operation? He also agreed.

Dr. Surgeon removed the breast lump and Dr. Tom
accepted the specimen at the door of the operating room.
Still gowned and gloved, we waited. Ten minutes. Twenty.
Dr. Surgeon cocked an eyebrow over the top of his mask.
Thirty. Then Dr. Tom reappeared, a grin apparent around his
surgical mask.

"All clear, benign."

He winked and motioned to us to follow him back to the
laboratory. "Blasted cryostat sprang a leak of refrigerant," he
said, "wouldn't freeze the specimen. No repairmen within
a hundred miles. So, Ray Critchley (our resident genius of
laboratory and x-ray technology) and I wheeled the machine
outdoors. Ambient temperature was minus 28 degrees. Cold
did its thing, and voila! A frozen specimen."

North country make-do; mission accomplished.

The Importance of a Pathology Report

At one of our twice-monthly hospital pathology
conferences, Dr. Tom waxed eloquent on the topic of studying
surgical specimens. His dictum: "If it's worth removing, it's
worth pathological examination. Period, end of discussion."

Yes sir.

A couple of days later, Mrs. Adamson came to my office
with a complaint of a malodorous vaginal discharge. I
examined her and discovered a long-overlooked tampon in
her vagina.

I was about to discard the offending artifact, then
remembered Dr. Tom's injunction. I grinned an evil smirk
and solemnly packaged up the sodden tampon, sending it off
to Duluth.

In due time, I received a formal pathology report. Dr.
Tom's diagnosis: "A clear case of cotton-picking syndrome."

To Hitch a Ride

Dr. Tom had a 7:30 a.m. date at one of the rural hospitals for which he served as a consultant. He left Duluth, headed east toward Wisconsin, at 5:30 on a brisk January morning. Translate brisk as twenty-five below zero. En route, a horrible noise erupted from a back wheel of the car. It proved to be almost red-hot. He managed to reach a service station and left the wounded vehicle. Traffic had been wintertime light. Finally, a loaded logging truck rounded a bend and Dr. Tom stuck out his thumb. He explains what happened next:

"Where you headed?" asked the driver as he began a series of gearshifts.

I told the man my destination, Dr. Tom said.

"Do you live there?"

"No, I live in Duluth."

"Oh, do you work out here?"

"Sometimes, like today." I dreaded the obvious next question; here it came.

He asked, "What do you do?"

"I'm a doctor."

He cocked an eyebrow. "Do you always hitchhike over here?"

"Well, you know, Medicare payments are really bad."

The man nodded. "Yah, I understand. The government will screw you every time."

We had a good, if kidney-jostling trip. Arrived in town, I told the man I could get out on the highway. He looked around, said, "I don't see any hospital."

It was several blocks away, I explained.

"Doc, it's too cold to walk. Hang on."

He swung that big rig and trailer around a narrow corner. When he chugged into the hospital driveway, he nearly clipped off part of the entrance canopy. He bade me a cheery goodbye and drove away to snarls from shifting gears and the hiss of airbrakes. I trudged into the hospital. A friend stood in the entrance, attracted by the growls a loaded logging truck makes. He rolled his eyes.

"You! What next?"

To Save a Soul

To understand my Norwegian friends and relatives, keep in mind that godliness is secondary only to stoicism. Words are suspect, for do they not sometimes bed down with . . . emotion?

A privilege of a country doctor is to know neighbors so well. I am minded of Olaf and Fredrick Anfinson, bachelor brothers from the "alt country." Norwegian fishermen.

Doctor Tom was the conveyor of this true tale about mutual friends.

Back in the 1940s, a church of uncertain denomination hatched a flock of zealous missionaries. A number of them undertook the onerous task of improving the spiritual life of those tough Lake Superior fishermen.

The Right Reverend Jimmy Bob Surely was a wooly bear of a man. He drove all the way up from Duluth one August day. He always wore a broad-rimmed hat. He carried a tattered Bible in one hand and a cane in the other.

The house which Olaf and Fredrick called home had been built by a fisherman from an earlier generation. Rough-hewn boards, rolled green roofing material for siding, squinty windows designed more for keeping cold outside than letting in light. Floors bounced underfoot. A hand pump set into the kitchen sink provided water with full modern convenience. No more hauling it up a bucketful at a time from The Lake.

It was about 2 p.m. on the day when Missionary Surely knocked at the screen door to Anfinson's house. A series of rattling thumps. Fredrick levered himself out of the armchair where he had been involved in a nap. He peered through rusty screen at the imposing figure on his doorstep. The big man took off his hat.

"Ja?" Fredrick said.

"Good afternoon, sir. I hope the day finds you well."

"Ja."

"Warm out here."

"Ja?"

"I wonder if I might have a few minutes of your time."

"Vell, I had in mind—"

"Of course, sir. Still, some things are so important that I dare cross the boundaries of constraint."

"Huh?"

"If I might come in?"

"Vell—"

"It's awkward speaking through this screen, especially about as important a topic as one's immortal soul."

"Your soul got trouble?"

Hearty chuckles shook the broad abdomen contained by the Right Reverend Jimmy Bob's trousers. "No, no, sir. Mine is accounted . . . that is, I had in mind one more important to you."

"Ja?"

"Yours, sir. If you might just unlatch the hook of your screen door."

"Vell—"

"Thank you, sir." The Right Reverend wrung Fredrick's hand and glanced around. "What an . . . interesting place."

"Oh, so?"

"May we be seated? Thank you. I hope I didn't steal your favorite chair."

"You did."

"Oh? Oh! I'll just sit over . . . tell me, what is your name?"

"Fredrick."

"And mine is the Right Reverend . . . uh, just call me Brother Jimmy Bob. What is your occupation?" The Right Reverend sniffed. "Well, fish do leave their . . . I can guess. And your denomination?'

Fredrick cocked an eyebrow. "I be a fella."

Brother Jimmy Bob grinned and waved his hands. "I meant your faith allegiance."

"Norvegian."

"No, no, what is your church affiliation?"

"Ohhh. Lut'ern."

"Of course, one of those. Which congregation do you belong to?"

Fredrick scratched his head. "Ve never choosed up sides."

"But you are Lutheran?"

"In general."

"Have you considered the state of your immortal soul?"

"State? Vell, ve vas from Tofte, alt country, but over here ve're Minnesota."

"No, no, I mean your spiritual state."

"Oh, ja, that probably be the same."

"I don't believe I'm making myself clear."

"You be right dere."

Brother Jimmy Bob waved his Bible with enough vigor to flutter its pages. He roared like Moses on the mount, "Do you know Jesus Christ?"

"Noooo. You need go down to the fish house and talk to my brother, Olaf. He knows everybody on the whole North Shore."

Time caught up with Olaf Anfinson, hardening of the arteries and heart disease, diabetes. He was brought to the hospital one day, in heart failure and declining kidney function. He expired within the week.

A friend saw Fredrick a few days later and said, "I understand you buried Olaf last week."

Fredrick replied, "Had to. Died."

• • •

My Fellow Americans

"My fellow Americans . . . " Hmm. That has a nice ring to it. No wonder politicians are so intoxicated by it. Still, it is a reminder of what benefits we all share.

If I might borrow from and paraphrase Mr. Art Linkletter: People say . . . and do . . . the darnedest things! We Americans are so diverse. Character and attitude, courage and yes, genes, determine health in more than subtle ways. Of the many joys I gained from a rural practice, what warmed me regularly was the opportunity to know my neighbors so well. Consider the following keyhole glimpses of fellow Minnesotans:

To most Americans, mention of Minnesota conjures images of "Yah sure, you betcha," Scandinavians. Swedes, Norwegians, Finns and a few Danes. Native son Garrison Keillor is wildly popular beyond the boundaries of our state. His tales do nothing to discourage the perception. Demographers tell a different story. Droves of Germans, farmers mostly, settled in the southern half of Minnesota, and their numbers gained pre-eminence.

Dr. Robert P. Meyer, M.D., is himself a descendent of German settlers. He relates a vignette from his own experience:

The congregation of a small Lutheran church located a few miles from his home in Faribault, Minnesota, met to discuss a dilemma. Should sermons be conducted comfortably in Deutsch, or in this difficult new language of English? Debate proceeded ponderously. "Do you want us to understand Pastor?" asked the gray-hairs. "Do you want to be old country?" demanded radical youths. Finally, Herr Reinhart labored to his feet from an honored seat in the front pew. The angry buzz died, out of respect for Der Alte.

"The thing comes down," he said, in German, "to Mrs. Guenther. She has to play the organ. I ask you now, can she make sense of a good German hymn, playing it on an American organ?"

Pastor Johnson folded long legs to the demands of a short-legged chair. Time for the children's sermon. He surveyed his flock of fuzzy-headed chicks and held up the prop he had chosen for the day.

"Can anyone tell me what this is?"

Billy T. waved frantically. Pastor nodded at him.

"A telephone," Billy chirped.

Pastor beamed. "Who calls us on the telephone?"

Sally took her thumb out of her mouth long enough to say, "Gran'ma."

"And Bobby!" screamed Joseph.

"Right. People. Does God use this to call us?"

"No, 'cause it ain't plugged in," said Billy T.

"Well, assume it was, what then?"

Billy T. rested his chin on a pudgy forefinger, then brightened. "God don't call collect."

Oscar drove ambulance for the local hospital, a volunteer. He wore a pager and had just invested in a cell phone. He hung it on his belt beside the pager.

It was a chilly afternoon. He wore a windbreaker jacket, snug at wrists and waist.

He decided to try out his new-fangled toy, reached for the telephone. It had vanished! He whirled around. Not lying obviously in view. Dang! He retrieved his pager and on some hunch of frustration punched in the number of his phone.

It jangled from inside his constricting jacket. "Made me jump like a cricket on a griddle," he told me. "Dang thing fell off the belt and slid down far as the elastic at the bottom of the jacket."

Summer Bible camp held eight-year-old Martha in thrall. Hours spent in hot, airless tents, confined to hard folding chairs, had crammed her freewheeling spirit into too tight a binder. Time came for the kiddies to act out their Bible verses. Martha bobbed up on wire-spring legs and declaimed,

"If someone smiteth you on one cheek, smiteth them back on the other."

Overheard at the eye doctor's office:

Receptionist: "Good morning, madam. You insisted there was a dire emergency when you called in. What can we do for you?"

Buxom, middle-aged lady: "I lost my glasses."

"Oh dear. When?"

After a moment of thought: "Eight months ago."

I have a friend; call him Milt. He is ten or fifteen years younger than I. He retired a few years ago to a life of well-earned leisure. His passion is fishing, and he is honored by acclamation as one of the North Shore's most knowledgeable at the sport. Milt is a local boy, born and bred, and Ojibwe heritage earns him solid privilege to title of Original Settler.

The iron ore known as taconite is refined and homogenized into marble-sized pellets before shipment east from Minnesota ports, through the chain of Great Lakes to steel mills in Ohio and Pennsylvania. Milt worked at the ore loading dock a few miles west of town.

One day Milt was helping to load an ore carrier. The process is largely automatic, involving huge conveyer belts capable of filling the holds of a thousand-foot-long boat in a few hours. Milt stood on top of a closed hatch cover, monitoring the loading process. He realized the boat shifted slightly when prodded by lazy Lake Superior swells and began to shift his weight from one leg to the other in time with the ponderous movements.

A nearby sailor cocked any eyebrow. "Hey Chief, what ya doin'?"

"Rain dance," Milt said solemnly. "Been dry."

He told me what happened next.

"Doc, it was a warm, bright sunny day and Lake Superior was as blue as the sky. Man, it wasn't fifteen minutes later when I looked up and by gar, from behind the loading bins

38

roared the dang darkest, wildest clouds I saw all summer. Rain came down like from out of a hydrant. I tipped my hard hat at the sailor and did a fast two-step Indian dance on my way to cover. You know, I'd give a week's pay to know what that sucker told everyone when he got back to Cleveland."

A Wink and a Grin

Courage is the bright shield of the human spirit. More than most people, a country doctor is privileged to see it close at hand. When I think of examples of special courage, Brad smiles back at me.

I don't recall my first encounter with Brad. A childhood immunization? Some viral infection? He had arrived in town with his mother and two sibs, just one of Eunice's children. She had left her husband behind in the far away metropolis where they had previously lived. Why had Eunice chosen Northpine? If I once knew, I have forgotten.

In a community the size of mine, free-floating local gossip supplies part of that background information on which a country doc depends, relationships, family schisms, stresses— character forming events, healthy or detrimental. Brad's father was said to have been a professor at a college where avant-garde opinion held sway. He had purposely introduced his children to the glories of psychedelic drugs, in the form of LSD.

Brad became memorable to me when he was about sixteen. He was a strong rangy lad, darkly handsome.

To an isolated country doctor, office hours provide merely the structured part of his practice. Emergency call . . . nights, weekends, holidays . . . presents a more chaotic side to professional life. Thus it was that I was summoned to the hospital emergency room about ten that evening. Brad had been brought in by his mother. A pair of uneasy youths restrained him by the arms. He muttered steadily, random words and mere sounds, word salad. He twitched in constant motion, jerking his head from side to side, picking at clothing or at unseen specters around him.

Anguish tightened Eunice's features and she tortured interlaced fingers. "They called from school this afternoon," she said in a monotone. "I brought him home, but I think he's getting worse. I can't manage . . . it's the way he was

40

before when he took . . . I think he got into more LSD." Her eyes sought mine, parent's eyes pleading for understanding, eyes unable to hide fear and pain. "Don't send him to a crazy hospital! He'll sleep it off, he has before."

Northpine was not the center of a drug culture. I acceded to Eunice's request, ordering my uneasiness to be still, and admitted Brad to our tiny hospital. We had one room that could be locked up. The nurses and I draped the boy in a patient gown, got him into bed, and turned the key. I departed for the doctor's lounge and a crash conference with my medical textbooks on how to ease someone down from a bad trip.

During the night, he shredded linen and disassembled his bed, including nuts and bolts, without benefit of a tool. We cleaned out debris and eased him onto a bare mattress laid on the floor.

During the next few hours, he showed no aggression toward staff members. Rather, he ignored us, tuned as he was to inner visions. Endless muttering. Vacant eyes. Constant, restless motion. The tears shed were by his family; he remained insulated within the murky universe of chemistry. Toward noon, he retreated into an almost vegetative state, curled up on his mattress.

Then . . .

The nurses called me just after twelve-noon. When they tried to feed him, he abruptly got up from his mattress and marched determinedly down the corridor, a pair of nurses dragging behind him like too-small boat anchors on a windy day. I arrived and latched onto the tails of his patient gown. I was no match for Brad's strength. He pushed open the emergency side door and headed down the steep hill toward town. I dug in my heels.

"Brad! Stop!"

I was talking to the wind.

"Someone call the police," I screeched over my shoulder.

November in my Northpine is chilly. I was in shirt sleeves, but I at least wore trousers and shoes. Wearing that far away look that excluded me, Brad strode on. One block. Two. A

41

squad car and two policemen arrived. Burly lads. We steered Brad toward the backseat of the car.

It was obviously time to set aside any question of "letting him sleep things off in Northpine." I sent him to a psychiatrist in Duluth, where Brad began the long climb out of a drug-induced psychosis.

A country doctor has what I consider both an advantage professionally and a joy personally. He sees his patients over an extended time. Brad returned home finally. Flashbacks waned, and he reintegrated himself into family and the community. We talked at length. He had no recollection of his stay in our hospital, nor of many of his days in Duluth. He decided that drugs carried for him a risk beyond acceptance. So far as I know, he never chanced another LSD trip. He buttressed determination by involving himself in Northpine's active, effective AA program.

I like to think that whenever we met, his greetings, ever a wink and a grin, meant a special bond between us. I know how I felt.

Brad died a couple of years ago. He was a logger, used to hard work, and he had not "fallen off the wagon." It is presumed that he had had a heart attack at the appallingly young age of fifty.

With permission of his family, I tell Brad's story in a spirit of tribute. I have known few people during my years in medicine who fought harder, against a demon more relentless, and who succeeded better than did Brad. I cherish memory of that private, special wink and grin.

DR. NORMAN HAGBERG, M.D., CONTRIBUTED THE NEXT THREE STORIES

Dr. Norman Hagberg, M.D., served his southwestern Minnesota community as a Family Physician for decades. He epitomized what Country Doctor means to those who relied on such for skillful, compassionate care. I am pleased to introduce Dr. Hagberg through reminiscences from his own practice:

The Staff of Life

Olga suffered a stroke. It resulted in significant swallowing problems. Despite this handicap, nurses and aides at the local nursing home carefully and patiently provided her with adequate nutrition, so as to avoid a feeding tube.

The biggest problem the staff faced was that her husband, Ole, insisted on feeding her bread, causing her to choke on several occasions. The nurses asked me to speak to him regarding the bread, as their requests had gone unheeded.

I knew this could be a touchy challenge because I had observed his "short fuse" in the past. Ole was a stubborn old Scandinavian who lived by the premise that his way was the only way.

Ole and Olga had been former neighbors of mine, providing some common ground for conversation. I arranged to meet with Ole at the nursing home one morning. We reminisced about the past, how I had enjoyed watching him plow and cultivate his small field with a miniature John Deere tractor. Its two-cylinder, putt-putt engine still left great acoustical memories. I reminded him of how much my five children had frequented their front door, Olga always ready with treats. "She had them believing marshmallows grew in her garden!"

With a few more old stories and laughs, I felt that I had developed good rapport. I explained to him that Olga's stroke had caused swallowing difficulties and that she should have only pureed or very soft food. I said she should not be fed bread—

It was as if the word BREAD lit a torch and his mood switched one hundred and eighty degrees. He stiffened and leaned toward the bedside stand between us. His eyes flashed, his face flushed, and veins in his neck stood out like ropes. He pound his fist on the table in rhythm with his words.

"BREAD IS THE STAFF OF LIFE, AND BY GOD SHE'S GOING TO HAVE BREAD!"

Shortly thereafter, Olga succumbed to the ravages of her stroke—hopefully without a chunk of bread stuck in her throat.

Endless Love

I knocked on hospital room 106 before entering.

Charlie was sitting at his wife's bedside with her hand clasped in his. Their sixty-plus years of marriage appeared to me as perfect bliss. We had some conversation, and he, knowing I had to examine her, excused himself. He slowly raised himself from his chair, leaned over to kiss his wife and said goodnight. Cane in hand, he shuffled toward the door.

She called to him, "Now, you be good."

He slowly turned in a robot-like manner, winked at me and said, "That gets easier all the time."

Maple Nut Ice Cream

Emil walked briskly into my examination room. As always, he was accompanied by his wife, Mabel, twenty-plus years younger. He was a small man with a deep voice and was unusually alert and spry for being one hundred years old. Emil always dressed in a white shirt and dark trousers, held in place by suspenders. I had seen him as a patient many times over the previous twenty-five or more years.

His first, and only, marriage had been to Mabel at the age of sixty-five. He was a very pious man and invariably on every office visit would give testimony to his Maker, but always in an inoffensive manner.

One day I asked him how he accounted for his one hundred years. He smiled. "I have a bowl of maple nut ice cream every night before bed."

His wife chimed in, "You should come out some evening for ice cream. And, he loves to play Chinese checkers. He always beats me."

Not long afterward, I had a night free of emergency call. It was a gorgeous mid-summer evening, so I rode my bike to their home, seven miles out in the country. It was one of those perfect Minnesota evenings, a lazy sun dipping toward the west, with a nice south breeze at my back. Bicycling gives time to muse. It had been a wonderful day, starting with an early-morning delivery of a beautiful baby.

I knocked on the front door of their quaint little white frame house. Both Emil and Mabel met me inside. He always addressed me as "Doctor" in a very proper and respectful manner. After shaking hands, he grabbed me by the arm and led me to the Chinese checker table. While I was getting beat for the second time, I remembered his wife telling me, "He loves to play checkers."

With the game ended and a gleam in his eyes, Emil asked, "Another?"

I said, "How about that maple nut ice cream?"

Mabel dished it up and the three of us sat at their little kitchen table. Emil said, "We shall pray." In his deep, theatrical voice he began, "Thank you, Lord for . . ."

My attention wandered. I thought, "Wow! If two dips of ice cream rate this long a prayer, what about a whole meal?" Then I plugged back in.

" . . . and lastly, Lord, thank you especially that Dr. Hagberg came to see us."

My throat tightened and my eyes teared.

We enjoyed our small talk and ice cream and I was soon on my way home. I peddled leisurely with one finger on the tip of the handle bar, soaking up the beauty of the countryside. The setting sun cast shadows on waving, golden wheat in one field, and in another, corn was "Field of Dreams" high.

I thought to myself, "I have the best job in the world as a family physician. Thank you, Lord, for the many Emils and Mabels I have come to know, who have entrusted their medical care to me!"

• • •

Randolph Zimmer

Northerners are a special breed. Pioneer ancestors of
European descent arrived in our area only three generations
ago. Their strengths persist in their descendents. Courage.
Independence. An acceptance of life and its rigors. Randolph
was a son of the North.

Randolph was forty-seven when I first met him. He
worked for a local contractor, drove trucks, helped with
cement work, operated heavy equipment. He was a handy
fellow to have around.

One day he arrived in the emergency room of the
community hospital. "Hit by a car," explained Millie, our
peppery outpatient nurse. "The dang fool didn't jump out of
the way quick enough."

I sidled next to the gurney on which Randolph lay. A
scratch on his cheek, a bruised hand. A tear in his work shirt
would require more stitches than he himself.

"What happened?" I asked.

"You the new doc? I'm Randy. Crossin' Broadway, on my
way to the bank, next I knew there was Herb Smith in his new
Ford, bearin' down like one them avalanches you read about.
A'fore I could get out the way, he skidded into me and set me
on my rump."

I did those things a doctor does when a car bumps a body,
no matter how gently. Found the promise of more bruises. An
abrasion of an elbow. No sign of serious injury. To be sure, I
ordered x-rays of his hips and back. Films showed working-
man-sturdy bones free of obvious trauma.

"Can you walk?" I asked.

"Sure. Since I was so high." He held his hand low.

I winced, grinning. "Set you up for that, didn't I?
Why don't you show me?"

He eased off the gurney, steadied himself with one hand
for a moment before walking carefully across the emergency

room. He put a hand against the wall, turned with cautious shuffles of his feet, and walked back.

"Sore?" I asked.

His face remained placid, but I caught a twinkle in his eye. "Doc, you ever had a Ford park you on your ass?"

His wife had arrived to take Randolph home. We shook hands. I watched him walk along the hallway toward the exit. He walked—carefully. Shuffled, actually.

Stoical men of Randolph's stripe do not casually visit a doctor. I did not see him in the office during the next couple of years. That explained why I belatedly made my diagnosis of Randolph's medical condition in Johnson's Food Market. I was in the aisle devoted to the competitive world of breakfast cereal. He waved at me when I called his name, scratched his head, then reached for a box of corn flakes. He paused in contemplation of choices and his hand began to shake, a tremor that could be described as rolling, a back and forth motion. Yet, when he took the cereal from its place, the action was coordinated enough to do what he needed. He trudged ahead of me, reached the end of the aisle at the back of the store—and walked into the meat counter. He pushed away and vanished from my view around the end of the aisle.

The mental gears required to make a diagnosis whirred. A facial expression I had considered stoicism, blank and devoid of those little twitches we all carry about as unconscious baggage. A tremor at rest, which doctors have termed pill-rolling. Like a linguistic fossil, the phrase is from a past when physicians did in fact roll medications into pills. A gait characterized by shuffling feet, a slightly forward-tipped posture, as though he was constantly a fraction of a step behind his center of balance. Characteristically, decreased ability to stop once he embarked in one direction. No wonder, as nurse Millie had remarked those years before, that he was unable "to jump quick enough."

From what I saw that day in Johnson's Market, I was prepared to diagnose Randolph as suffering from Parkinson's disease. Splendid—and only two years belatedly.

Parenthetically, I now faced a familiar dilemma. Every so

48

often a doctor identifies an obvious medical condition while engaged in a social situation. A mole that looks suspicious for melanoma, a bump on someone's cheek that could well be a basal cell carcinoma. An obviously enlarged lymph node. A swollen thyroid gland. Someone whose skin is clearly jaundiced. Behavior crying out, "chemical dependency." A man with Parkinson's disease! To emulate Sir Galahad and charge in with an unsolicited diagnosis can result in more than embarrassment. I speak from experience.

I stewed in private.

The passage of time—a few months, as I recall—and I was able to address Randolph's condition directly. He fell off his porch when that inability to stop brought him too close to its edge. His wife had the resolve to override Randolph's objections and used the minor accident as an excuse to get him back to my office.

I worked up Randolph fully, had him consult a neurologist, and then began the use of those few drugs that relieve the worst symptoms of the miserable disease. More time passed.

The University of Minnesota Medical School launched an innovative educational program in 1970. Named Rural Physician Associate Program, or more affectionately, R-PAP, its thrust was to persuade graduates to forego the comfort of a city practice and locate where doctors were desperately needed, in rural Minnesota. I agreed to play a role. The process involved placing a third-year medical student in the office of a selected rural physician for from nine to twelve months. The student and physician/preceptor worked together daily. A feature involved periodic rural site visits from university faculty members, top experts each in his or her field. This bonus for the local doctor allowed a free evaluation of four or five confusing cases from his practice.

Randolph deteriorated gradually. His tremors became debilitating, he had to quit working, drugs became less effective, and he began to exhibit bizarre mental behavior. The traditional concept of Parkinson's disease is that mentation is usually unaffected. He was a conundrum.

As medical students arrived in my office over the next three years, each for a year's exposure to "the real world of medicine," we scheduled the visiting university neurologist to consult in Randolph's case.

Three high-octane neurologists—three different diagnoses.

It is sometimes disconcerting to patient-type folks to discover that doctors are people too, afflicted with opinions and blind spots. Even experts boasting more credentials than Minnesota does mosquitoes are not immune. Disagreements between really expert experts can become—let's say, rancorous. (Maybe you didn't know that.) After all these consultations, with Randolph as their focus, my compulsive search for truth ended up causing his family more confusion than comfort.

The grim disease holding Randolph in its grip ran its course, and he eventually died. I sat down with his survivors, I as bemused as were they. I telephoned the one university expert who had opted for a diagnosis of Parkinson's disease, explained our frustrations. He offered the services of the university. If the family would allow an extraordinary autopsy, one in which the entire nervous system, brain and spinal cord, were removed intact, he would see that their pathology department did a thorough examination of the tissues.

His family agreed.

At long last we learned what had caused Randolph, and indirectly the rest of us, such a difficult time. Randolph had indeed died of Parkinson's disease. In the same sense that Lou Gehrig's name became associated with amyotropic lateral sclerosis, or ALS, perhaps we might today consider Parkinson's disease as Pope John Paul's disease.

The illness is caused by a gradual destruction of specialized cells in the basal ganglia of the brain. In less formidable terms, this part of the nervous system is one of its most primitive. Animals far down the tree of life possess the same essential cells. Coordination and agility are ancient requirements for existence.

Is there no hope for such patients?

Well . . .

Parkinson's is one disease for which stem cells, those magical "uncommitted" cells that appear at the very beginning of life, show promise. A stem cell can be steered into a developmental pathway that results in healthy replacement cells of the kind that hold the disease at bay. After nurturing in a laboratory dish, they in turn can be "planted" in a person suffering from the disease. A cure! The technology involved lurks just beyond a near horizon.

Why is this life-saving treatment not today being vigorously investigated?

Ask politicians.

DR. KENNETH CARTER, M.D., CONTRIBUTED THE NEXT THREE STORIES

Dr. Kenneth Carter, M.D.—Doctor Ken, as he is known to most of his patients—is an experienced physician, certified by the American Academy of Family Physicians. He grew up on a farm in northwestern Minnesota and graduated from the University of Minnesota Medical School with an M.D. degree in 1968. He has practiced in Granite Falls, Minnesota, since 1970. Some of the hats he wears include that of a Family Physician, with a focus on geriatrics. He serves as Yellow Medicine County coroner, medical director of Granite Falls Hospice and as Granite Falls Home Care Director. Please meet Dr. Carter through stories from his practice:

Frieda Schultz

Frieda was eighty-five that day. I knew that her husband of so many decades was eighty-six. She had been a regular visitor to my office. A bun of gray hair perched on the back of her neck. Years of sun and wind had creased her face. Her frame was lean, her limbs angular, and arthritic fingers were as gnarled as burls on a forest oak. Her cotton dress was homemade, lines stark, some nameless dark shade. Its hem reached mid-calf. Frieda Schultz wore the proper uniform of a southern Minnesota farm wife.

I sat before her, attentive.

"It's that Arthur-itis again," she said.

"Where is it acting up this time?" I asked.

"Knees."

I leaned forward and palpated the bumpy joints. "Sore?"

"Not to that. Hurts to walk and wakes me up at night."

I went through the litany of treatment that arthritis invokes: warmth, rest-plus-exercise of a gentle sort, aspirin or ibuprofen. Her somber features did not relent.

Something more? So often a declared "symptom" is merely

a ticket to gain a doctor's attention.

I asked, "How are things going at home?"

She looked at me full on. "Terrible! My John doesn't love me anymore."

"How have you decided that?"

"He hasn't wanted to make love with me for six months."

Ah. Some human needs have no expiration date. I leaned forward again and touched her arm gently.

"It may help to remember that John is eighty-six, and diabetic. There are things a man really can't help." I explained about the disease and its erosive effects on masculine performance. "From what I've seen of him," I said, "I find it hard to believe that he has quit loving you. Maybe a little patience on your part?" She nodded tentatively. "A little, uh, help from you?"

She nodded briskly. Her smile was as bright as all outdoors on a sunny day. She bobbed up and strode to the door. Her knees seemed to have discovered renewed strength and vigor.

I dictated on her chart and paused, bemused. Should I call John, a friendly alert?

Clinton

The thing about starting a practice somewhere is that . . . it has to start sometime, somewhere. I was new to medicine and new to the community, a village of four hundred people. That comfort which experience bestows must be earned the hard way. I hoped that the confidence I donned each day was not too obviously brand new.

Incessant ringing of the doorbell to my home awoke me one night at 2:30 a.m. I stumbled downstairs and opened the front door. Two elderly gentlemen seized the front of my pajamas, both talking at once.

"Clinton lives next door to me . . . " shouted one.

"He's been out deer hunting and . . . " chimed in the other.

"Spent the evening at the Powerhouse Tavern, stumbled

home after they expelled him . . . "

"Fell out his own bathroom window, been running amok ever . . . "

" . . . since and he's scaring everybody. Figured you should come."

I asked where he was at the moment.

"Back alley, half block west."

"Can't you hear him, Doc?"

I pried myself loose, threw on enough clothes that I wouldn't be arrested myself, and decided to drive my car into the dark alley, using its headlights for illumination.

My proud doctor's satchel still bore its original coat of polish. I had stocked it with nearly as many supplies as the City Drug Store downtown. Heavy. I positioned the car to shine beams along the alley. Clinton lay against Johnson's garage. Several neighborhood men had attached themselves grimly to assorted parts of the lad's anatomy. If they were winning the fight to hold Clinton down, it was not obvious.

I popped open my medical case and drew a dose of intravenous sedative into a syringe. I edged close to the pile of twisting arms and legs. Clinton kicked a leg free on the precise moment I held my syringe at the ready. Sedative and all, it soared away into darkness. Gone. I groped in my bag of tricks again. Thorazine, a drug used to quiet a psychotic patient— when there is no alternative.

The men sitting on Clinton subdued him enough that I was able to slip a needle into an arm vein. I learned that the drug also works on a rambunctious drunk; quiet and peace returned to our dark alley.

I had a moment to contemplate the situation. Here I was, as far from orderly Academia as the north pole is from the south, with an unconscious young tough who could awaken at any moment. No one during training had told me that medicine might be so confrontational!

By then, town constable Fred Johnson had arrived. Fred drove an old station wagon which, with the back seat laid flat, could carry a stretcher. Fred was our town's law, and also its entire ambulance squad. If Clinton awoke on the way to the nearest hospital, located in a town ten miles away, both Fred and our patient would be at risk.

There was no built-in means of securing Clinton to the stretcher. Looking for something to immobilize the lad, we found a fifty-foot electric cord in a nearby garage. We wound cord around him and the stretcher until he could have passed for a mummy. Fred headed for Our Sisters of Peace Hospital, I following in my own car. En route, Clinton slept as quietly as a hound pup dreaming in the sun.

He awoke toward suppertime. I poked my head cautiously around the jamb of his hospital room when I called to recheck him. It pays to use circumspection; one never knows. When he spied me, Clinton had the good grace to blush clear to his toes.

I was only weeks away from my internship, and medical school curriculum is encyclopedic. Still, I couldn't recall having had a course in Subduing Wild Patients in a Dark Alley in the Middle of the Night - 101. Maybe I had just finished the course. Got a passing grade, then.

Until Death Do Us Part

Glacial-till landscape, gently-rolling hills and broad fields, characterize southwestern Minnesota. It is the eastern edge of our country's Great Plains. The terrain offers little hindrance to violent weather. Many of Minnesota's worst winter storms roar out of Canada from the northwest. We call them Alberta Clippers, furies that can pounce with little warning.

I received a call from the community hospital. A woman in labor. I drove through howling snow that was rapidly forming drifts. Sometime after midnight, I welcomed our newest citizen into the world.

When I pushed open the hospital door to head for home, kernels of snow riding winds as cross as Old Man Simmons during one of his gout attacks slammed me in the face. Like peering into the maw of a sandblaster. Discretion did its thing,

55

and I headed back into the hospital. A night spent on the atrocity called the doctor's-lounge bed seemed a better choice than heading for home.

The storm abated along about noon and I headed out again, visions of a nap dancing in my head.

The telephone rang at 3 p.m. I was county coroner, and yes, Sheriff Robertson, I was available. The next town north? On my way.

I arrived at the scene and found rescue-squad and county law-enforcement personnel waiting. They plopped me onto a sled pulled behind a snowmobile and wrapped me to my ears. The machine growled past a venerable farmhouse, across open fields for more than half a mile. We stopped next to a small knot of officers, huddled against winds still pushing loose snow into swirling snow devils.

I have noticed that whenever professionals must attend a found body, they stand in an awkward circle, looking everywhere but at the death that summoned them. Almost as though apologetic for still breathing in the presence of one who never will again.

I crawled out of the cocoon that had been constructed for me on the sled and knelt beside—the bodies of two elderly people lay huddled together in a cradle of snow. A man and a woman.

"Al Johnson," Sheriff Robertson said somberly, "and Bess, his wife. Both widowed, they've only been married three or four years. Bess was blind, but old Al there took care of her so well that she never wanted. Damn shame."

"What happened?" I asked. "How'd they manage to get clear out here?"

"Had to have walked. Imagine, that wind and cold last night. They'd been out to supper at the Wayside Café. When they started for home, it wasn't that bad yet, but you know these Clippers. Al made it as far as the beginning of their driveway when the car stalled in snow. Must have figured they could make it that last hundred yards to the house. Set out, anyway. Near as we can figure, Al must have been guided more by the wind than by what he should have seen. 'Course, Bess being blind, she couldn't have helped. Doc, they missed the grove of windbreak trees around the house and barnyard by only twenty yards. So damn close, but so damn—"

"Yeah," I said.

Al and Bess. Each past eighty. They had struggled across arctic terrain for more than a mile. I tried to imagine it, then tried even harder to scrub the picture from my mind.

The nature of being a country doctor, of being a coroner, is that you see frozen bodies every so often. It's odd about people who have died of exposure. They look so . . . so as though all they have to do is wake up, crawl to their feet, and we can all go and have a beer while we laugh about the whole episode.

Al and Bess stick in my mind. Side by side, locked in icy permanence. What I never will forget is how tightly they still held hands.

• • •

Potpourri

G. L. had a unique ear problem. His hearing would diminish gradually, and a sensation as of water in the ear canal increased. I discovered that a layer of epidermis had thickened and begun to separate. Every six months, using a diminutive grasping tool called an alligator forceps, I would catch the outer edge of the detaching skin and could then tease out a perfect cast of his ear canal and drum, intact. Both ears. Reminded me of the skin a growing snake periodically discards. As I eased out the epidermal cast, he always beamed and said, "Ahhhhhh!"

I wonder if the snake felt the same way.

The larger a medical facility, the easier a patient's full needs may not be met.

I was still an intern. St. Lukes Hospital in Duluth, Minnesota, was taller than any other building within view. The delivery room was located on its top floor, where a large window faced the northeast. In Duluth, that meant the scene was a panorama of mighty Lake Superior.

A woman in labor is remarkably concentrated on what she is doing. Even placement in that position of indignity known as "in stirrups" becomes secondary to the primal task she faces. Endure labor's contraction when it comes, grasp a shred of rest when it relents. Still, she is not rendered deaf. To doctors and nurses waiting for baby's arrival, there is little to do but watch. Their conversation can seem uninvolved with pending events.

Mrs. Jones was perhaps half an hour away from delivery. The time was 5 a.m., the month June. The new day's sun in all its chromatic glory peered across Lake Superior at us where we medics stood, gowned, gloved and waiting. Red streaks warmed to gold. A fluff of cloud captured color in its white net. Water clear as the sky above it reflected a twin that was the sun's image. For the moment forgetting Mrs. Jones, lying with her all presented to God and us, I stared out the window at nature's canvas and said reverently, "I never tire of this view."

Mrs. Jones heard me.

I apologized to the lady. Explained frantically. The next day brought her a rose nearly as red as my face. She probably will have forgotten me, but after these sixty years, I haven't forgotten her.

"Don't use your head, gotta use you feet."

—*My Father*

Meningitis is always a serious disease. Some cases caused by viruses heal with few if any long term consequences. Bacterial infection of the meninges, the membranous envelope surrounding and protecting the nervous system, is always a disaster.

At the time of my internship in 1947, the most devastating diagnosis was meningitis caused by tuberculosis. It was one hundred percent fatal.

Each intern served one month on the infectious disease ward of the hospital. We spent our shifts enveloped in totally wrap-around contagion gowns, caps and masks. Only eyes and an inch of forehead showed. Constant scrubbing and the use of rubber gloves protected our hands.

Three-year-old Chip had been on the contagion service for three or four months when I arrived. He had been diagnosed with tubercular meningitis. The antibiotic streptomycin had been discovered shortly before. It killed the tough bug causing tuberculosis. Eventually.

There is a phenomenon called blood/brain barrier. Infections and drugs that perfuse freely about the rest of the body via the circulation are usually prevented from passing directly into the brain. Nature guards her most precious organ fiercely. Once breached, however, as had happened with young Chip, this same barrier prevents streptomycin, the curative drug he so desperately needed, from entering his nervous system in quantities sufficient to conquer the disease.

Chip's treatment involved performing a daily spinal tap

to inject antibiotic directly into his spinal fluid, where the infection smoldered.

Try to imagine what Chip's world had become. Everyone who approached him wore nightmare garb, even his parents. He lay caged in a crib made of iron bars. "Healers" manhandled him into a legs-to-chest position to force a curve in his back before plunging a hideously long, sharp needle into his spine, already sore from previous "treatments." Solutions of streptomycin that certainly must have hurt were injected into his spinal fluid. Daily! For month upon month.

Chip made medical history.

So far as his physicians could find, he was the first person ever to survive tubercular meningitis!

Chip became the mascot of the entire hospital staff. The day he went home, we all assembled—unmasked!—at the emergency room exit to wave, hug him, shower him with flowers and candy. His smile was as weak as a northern sun at winter solstice, but I would like to think he forgave us.

Chip, wherever you are, we cared.

Humor is the soul of humility.

The hospital intern on obstetrics circumcised the male babies. No alternative to the procedure was considered in 1947. A nurse tied three to ten squalling lads onto little wooden restrainers. Torture racks. The intern worked his way along the lineup, spreading joy with clamp and scalpel.

The Jewish community of Duluth used St. Lukes Hospital for their medical needs. When one of their little fellows arrived—what a difference.

The Rabbi officiated.

I do not follow the Jewish faith, but during my internship year I tried never to miss a ritual circumcision. I confess, there was an element of professional jealousy. The Rabbi's technique was slicker. I consoled myself with the thought that he had been at it longer than I. Oddly, by the time I acquired an equivalent proficiency, I had begun to wonder if, aside from religious tradition, it was really a necessary operation. I mean, parts are present for a reason, right? Is there divine mandate to whack parts off or out simply because they are there? The profession went through that kind of nonsense with tonsils fifty years ago. A tonsilectomy by patient request! Really. It's awkward to admit that doctors can be guilty of fads, too. Okay, when in the neighborhood, a surgeon routinely removes a vermiform appendix without a blush. Prevents its becoming infected later. Call it a suitable exception.

But back to my account. The reason we interns were so faithful at attending Jewish circumcisions had nothing to do with faith.

It was the party! Wine and food and gemutlicheit. When I did a "circ," there was no audience, no religious blessing, no beaming parent, no libation or food. Just a bored nurse and a chorus of unhappy lads.

Sigh.

There is that in human beings which hungers and thirsts for relationships as much as for food and water.

—*Eric Berne*

Bronson was one of a kind.

My only contact with the man was shortly after he had jacked up his house, preparatory to putting a new foundation under it. Jacks slipped and the house landed atop Bronson.

A hat that I donned regularly during those years was that of county coroner. I can't say that I ever became blasé when confronted with the disasters fate inflicts on yielding human flesh. Still . . .

Shades of the Land of Oz.

Don't expect too much of human beings. We were created at the end of the week when God was tired and looking forward to a day off.

—*Mark Twain*

The lad was twenty-one years old. He had gone hunting with family members that cold November day, but became separated from them. His father found him the next morning, lying lifeless in a foot of snow. He had stripped down to Jockey under-shorts, his boots and other clothing scattered along last faltering steps. Had hypothermia come to feel like heat?

Then there was John, another who encountered hypothermia. Eleven, he and his father had tipped a canoe in icy Lake Saganaga. They clung to it until it drifted near shore. John and his father crawled through the shallows, onto a rocky beach. When Father helped his son to an upright position, the boy died instantly. Experts in hypothermia tell us that the victim should be warmed while in a recumbent position to avoid catastrophic disturbances in the heart's rhythm.

I have observed that around a university medical school and hospital, the ultimate crime is Being Wrong. Odd, given how strewn with blind alleys and miscalculations is the path to any break-through discovery.

Surgeon Dr. Bob reports this episode. Mr. Jones had been a county engineer. Road construction had been a major part of his job. Dr. Bob had operated on him for colon cancer, had removed half of the large bowel.

Mr. Jones came for his last follow-up office visit. He squinted down the long incision running top to bottom of his abdominal wall.

"Good," he said. "I like a straight scar."

Dr. Bob muffled a chuckle. No interest in what went on "under the hood?"

So are we judged.

During the length of mankind's history, how many innocents have suffered or died because of someone else's religious convictions?

Another of Dr. Bob's patients, Bertha M., had fallen, breaking her arm. She was in her late sixties, lived alone in a small apartment. He had admitted her to a local nursing home for a period of weeks until she was spry enough to again care for her own needs.

Dr. Bob made rounds to see her one Sunday morning. Her daughter, Jane, and son-in-law, Ralph, were visiting her. Dr. Bob heard the conservation as he was leaving Bertha's room.

Ralph asked, "Mother, let me adjust your radio. Do you want to hear the church service or the Twins baseball game?"

Bertha chirped, "Depends on who's preachin' and who's pitchin'."

Have you ever wondered what God must have done to be saddled with supervising our cantankerous species?

While taking a medical history, it is important to ask the right question. The problem is to know what the dang right question is. Friend Dr. Vern Olmanson, a fine family physician from St. Peter, Minnesota, wryly relates a case in point.

A young lad arrived in his office, complaining of nausea and severe cramps, with tenderness in the right lower part of his abdomen. The story fit an attack of appendicitis too well to ignore, so it was decided that conservatism stood on the side of taking a look inside his belly. At surgery, the appendix was normal and no other explanation for the lad's symptoms was obvious. When in the area, it is customary to remove the appendix to prevent future trouble.

A couple of days later, the boy had an enormous bowel movement, comprised of great wads of chewed bubble gum, swallowed residue from more than a dozen packages.

In medicine, the realm of possibilities is infinite.

Bubble gum? Must add to the list of standard questions, how much of the stuff have you swallowed lately?

First, do no harm.

—*Hippocrates*

A variety of variations on a basic theme of cardiac testing

are in vogue today. Stressing a heart in the safe confines of a cardiologist's office has the aura of respectability. Of safety. Sixty years ago, in the far woods where I first hung my shingle, "make-do" was the order of the day.

A majority of my patients worked in the woods. That translates into hard work, physically stressful, carried out in places remote from emergency medical care. After several men succumbed to heart attacks, I began to wonder if there might be any chance of predicting those who were candidates for trouble. I did some reading in my medical journals . . .

At mid-twentieth century, doctor's offices were located upstairs more often than not. Almost as though orthodoxy required the challenge of a taxing stairway.

My first three years plus in practice I spent with Dr. R. D. Hanover, M.D., an accomplished and experienced country doctor. Then, he moved to a nearby community, leaving me behind, alone. I inherited his office. As was customary, it too was reached by climbing a long wooden staircase. A test of endurance.

A test of endurance? Maybe . . .

On the premise that it might be better to provoke a heart attack within the confines of the only hospital/office complex within a wide area, rather than to let someone have his attack fifty miles out in the woods, I started trotting suspect patients up and down that long stairway. I attached EKG electrodes to the man's chest in advance, then watched anxiously from the top while Jim or Joe or Hank rumbled up and down those stairs a few times. It is permissible to call the system crude. After half a dozen trips, I would march Jim or Joe or Hank back to the treatment room and record an EKG. The process actually uncovered a couple of vulnerable fellows, and no one suffered any harm.

Still, benign angels must have watched over us northwoods doctors. And our patients.

Pastor Johnson perched beside his tender young flock for the Sunday children's sermon. "We are honoring Dr. Martin

Luther King, Jr. today," he said. "Can anyone tell me who he was?"

Six-year-old Josh waved a hand frantically. Pastor pointed at him.

"He was . . . he was Dr. Martin Luther King Senior's son!"

Millie had worked as a nurse in our tiny community hospital from its first days. Floor nurse. Emergency room nurse. In charge of sterilizing supplies. In those days, everyone wore as many hats as need demanded. Most often, she was also the circulating nurse during an operation. Her job was to supply Nancy or Marie, the scrub nurses, with extra instruments, sterile towels and sponges when asked for, and to tend to any needs of Donna, our anesthetist. At the conclusion of the operation, she counted the sponges used to make sure all were accounted for.

About Millie. I've described her elsewhere as peppery. No one messed with Millie. And I loved the heck out of her.

We had reached the conclusion of some abdominal operation that day. Millie assembled the 4-inch by 4-inch squares of absorbent gauze we call sponges, counting silently.

Nancy and I stripped obscuring surgical drapes off the slumbering patient and nestled a soft bandage over his new lace-up job.

"Hold it," Millie said.

"What?"

"We're short one sponge."

Oh no. There are few things a surgeon wants less to hear.

We counted them again, aloud, in unison. One short. We spread out every drape and towel in the room. Still one sponge short. I sighed.

A small metal tab is sewed into each surgical sponge. An x-ray will reveal its whereabouts, even if it has been left behind in an abdomen just sewn back together.

"Have Ray gown up and bring in his x-ray machine."

Mille prowled around the room. She stopped in front of me. "Lift your feet, RAM."

65

"I'm sure that it couldn't be—"

Pasted to the bottom of one of my shoes was the missing sponge.

Millie snapped, "I've told you and told you, your big feet were going to cause trouble someday."

Yes, ma'am.

During all those years in my office, when Maxine transcribed the thousands of pages of medical notes I had dictated, the chatter of her typewriter was as steady as rain on a metal roof. Yet, when I would claim her attention in the midst of the task, she would answer my question without a ripple in the flow of data traveling from earphones to her fingers through her remarkable brain. She was a wonder.

Every Tuesday afternoon, for seventeen years, I held office hours in a converted house in the hamlet of Taconite Harbor. (Converted: Landlord Erie Mining Company lined the walls of one bedroom with lead sheets so that an x-ray machine could be installed.) Peggy was the nurse during so many of those years.

One day Thor Olafson arrived in the arms of his mother for a six-month checkup. Baby-type, that is, although the lad exemplified my visions of his Viking ancestors, a chunk. Nurse Peggy carried Thor to that exam room holding the baby scale. She stripped him and laid him in its tray. Not being otherwise occupied at the moment, I wandered along after Mother, Peggy and Thor, carrying half a cup of cooling coffee.

Peggy jiggled the weights on the scale, everyone oohed over the reading and I decided to take advantage of Thor's momentary tranquility to listen to his heart and lungs. I set my coffee cup alongside the scale, pulled my stethoscope from around my neck and . . .

I have seen pictures of an Italian fountain in which the source of water is a flow from a little boy's authentically represented penis.

Yup.

Just as I leaned toward the lad, he released a gorgeous stream of crystalline urine. It arced high; I jumped back. Unimpeded, it continued on a path to land directly into my coffee cup. And stayed on course until the last limpid drop.

Mirth . . . no, hysteria . . . exploded from Mother and Peggy. I heard folks in the waiting room calling out whats and what happeneds. Nurse Peggy laughed so hard her ears turned crimson. Honest.

There really are turning points in a person's life. Events that change the way you look at things forever after. From that day on, I never asked a patient to pee in a cup without having the years peer over my shoulder, and I again marveled at master Thor's remarkable accuracy.

In a sense, life is a succession of hellos and goodbyes.

Dr. Wallace Smith—Wally to colleagues and just plain Doc to everyone else in town—had practiced medicine in our community for decades. We were close friends. Although he had all but retired, Wally helped me when I needed an extra pair of doctor-type hands during an operation.

Wally was twenty-five years my senior. Always robust, as he had aged his shape came to model itself after an upside-down pear. He invariably wore rather old-fashioned underwear, loose enough not to bind.

One day he scrubbed with me while we performed a vein-stripping for varicosities in a patient's leg. This is as prolonged a procedure as I ever did, often lasting three or more hours. All the while, the surgical crew stood in one place. (A challenge to our own leg veins!) We finished at last and Wally stepped back from the operating table.

"Now I can take care of a little detail." He reached down and pulled up those unique undies. They had slid down-slope during the procedure and encircled his ankles like hobbles. Hidden from view by his encompassing surgical gown, no one but he had noticed.

He grinned cheerfully.

Wally was unique. Genial. Perceptive. Unassuming. He loved the North Shore passionately. I once heard a friend ask him if he would like to come along on a day-trip to Duluth. Wally thought for a moment, then said, "No thanks. I've already been there."

Old age begins when aspirations lie all in the past.

Henry was a logger, and a sober, hard-working family man. He came to my office one day for relief of what doctors call a subungual hematoma. A finger caught in a car door, a hemorrhage trapped under a separated fingernail. Imagine medieval torture. Relieving the pressure causing such discomfort is easily accomplished by burning a small escape hole through the nail substance, which itself has no nerve fibers, using a red-hot piece of wire. (A straightened paperclip works magnificently. Easily the cheapest medical tool I ever bought.) Convincing a patient that my intentions were benign when I showed up with a glowing wire was another matter.

I did my thing with the hot paper clip, relieving the pressure under Henry's nail, then decided an x-ray to rule out a fracture of the end joint was justified. No broken bone, but . . .

A two-inch piece of wire lay buried in Henry's hand.

"When did that happen?" I asked. "And how?"

He scratched hair already raked on end by his woodsman's cap. "I don't know, Doc. 'Course, a logger's always gettin' little scratches. You sure there's somethin' in there?"

I pointed at the x-ray film. "That's not imaginary."

He wiggled his fingers. "What did you have in mind to do about it?"

"In general, doctors favor removing that kind of hardware."

He turned the hand over, front to back. "How do you do that?"

"I'd make an incision, locate one end of the wire, and slide it out."

"Cut it open, huh. Might slow a man down, I 'spose."

"You, not knowing the blamed thing was in there, I'd not

be cocky sure."

"Still." He made a fist. "Reckon I'll just leave it be."

Why not?

Peace is not a passive, but an active condition, not a negation, but an affirmation. It is a gesture as strong as war.

—*Mary Roberts Rinehart*

Veteran nursing assistant J.E. provides this true anecdote. Bernt's rugged body bore scars that a lifetime spent fishing on Lake Superior inflicts. At some point he had lost an eye. He wore a tasteful artificial eye for the benefit of those around him. People not in the know sometimes envision such a prosthesis as being like a small ping pong ball, set into the vacant orbit. In reality, it is a saucer-shaped little object with an eye of appropriate color and size imprinted onto its convex (outer) surface. It then simply fits beneath the person's eyelids and responds to movement of muscles left by the surgeon.

The time came when Bernt could no longer provide care for himself and he entered the local nursing home. He was cheerful in the way a stoic Norwegian enters such a forbidding realm as emotion, free of malice and easy to care for. The only problem Bernt ever gave the nursing staff was that he kept losing his china eye.

One evening when J.E. began to settle him for the night, she noticed that his eye socket was again empty. The fact was, as usual, news to Bernt. J.E. searched his bedside table, his covers. She went through the wastebasket, crawled under the bed. No eye. She sighed.

"Hop out of bed, Bernt, let me look underneath you."

He gathered his bib-like gown about himself and slid onto his feet. There it was!

"Can you image what a sight it was," J.E. says, "to see a good Norwegian sea-blue eye, staring back at me from smack in the middle of Bernt's buttock?"

I'm Sorry to Inform You

There are some tasks that repetition never makes easier. Arturo, a case in point.

Call him Arturo. He was thirty-six that warm, summer day. Like hundreds of fellow Minneapolitans, he decided to escape down-state heat by driving to Minnesota's famed North Shore. Lake Superior provided coolness, an unfailing air-conditioner. Looming cliffs and green slopes dipped their feet in deep waters so blue that sky and lake seemed twins.

Arturo's car was a soft-top roadster, a Buick Elektra model, robust and crimson. Arturo liked red. Color and brightness betokened his cheerful attitude toward life. He was single, a bachelor with a firm understanding of priorities. Freedom to roam. A good job that provided the means to enjoy what he cherished. He still lived with Mama, but not because he was a wimp. He had never seen a reason to move from home. Besides, Mama loved having someone to dote on. He considered it an obligation of sorts, what with Papa in his grave these ten years. Did it matter who benefited the more from such an arrangement?

Arturo's hair was black, still free of any prophetic gray. True, it was thinner than he would have liked on top. His complexion was dark, a reflection of Mediterranean heritage. His skin did not burn, even that silver-dollar-sized bald spot.

Arturo rode with the big Buick's top folded back. Those days when Minnesota allowed such a luxury were to be enjoyed; why else have a car that his cousin scornfully called a Mississippi River barge? He released the seatbelt, as confining as a corset, and drove casually, an arm across the back of the passenger seat. Arturo relaxed, in control.

Traffic was heavy after he left Duluth and headed northeast on two-lane U.S. Highway 61. It was August. Everyone and their cousin on the way north, know what I mean? He trod the brake pedal and frowned. Always some joker doing forty-five in a fifty-five zone, piling up a string of cars behind him like the tail of a fume-belching comet.

Finally the old guy in the lead turned off at some resort and cars speeded up. How many ahead? Five, maybe . . . yes, six. Behind him? More than he could see. Passing on a crowded, curving highway like this one . . . he shackled impatience, grinned and shrugged.

The procession came to one of those small towns that cling to the rocky slopes of the North Shore. Speed zone ahead, announced a DOT sign, as if anybody paid the slightest attention to that kind of—

Oh-oh!

The driver at the head of this train of cars, so interdependent, wanted to turn left. There was oncoming traffic. The first car stopped, its turn blinker hiccupping redly. Car number two braked. Number three came within six feet of the bumper of number two. By the time Arturo absorbed what was happening, he was nearly chewing the tail pipe of the car in front of him. He stole a glance in the rear-view mirror—

A heavy-duty pickup truck directly behind him had passed that critical point when stopping remained an option. Tires blackened pavement loudly. Still traveling at thirty-plus miles an hour, the truck slammed into the rear of Arturo's roadster, crashing it against the car in front of him.

Arturo's Buick ejected him like a stuntman fired from a circus cannon. He sailed twenty-seven feet before landing squarely on his head.

I arrived at the scene some thirty minutes later. The snarl of traffic stretched for nearly a mile, cars funneling past the site one at a time. I declared the obvious, that Arturo was dead. Don, the highway patrolman working the scene, had found a name and phone number in the man's wallet. Don, his fellow officer, the just-arrived mortician—all eyes turned toward me. I was faced with the task of notifying survivors.

I drew a deep breath, found a telephone and dialed the number listed in Arturo's papers. A woman answered.

First, identify the person on the other end of the line. "Are you Mrs.-----?" Then choose from a repertoire of openers.

("I have bad news for you. Your son . . .")

("Are you sitting down? Your son . . .")

("I'm terribly sorry to have to report to you that your son . . .")

I cannot remember which inane phrases I used to tell the lady that her only child had been killed, but I will never forget what happened once she comprehended the message. She screamed and dropped the telephone; I heard it bounce on the floor. From then on, for the next minutes, the next horrors of minutes, I listened to her wailing anguish from three hundred unbridgeable miles away. I hollered into the phone, pled with her to pick up the receiver, cursed my insensitivity, willed my words be returned to me. She did not come back on the line, and I eventually hung up.

Dear unknown lady, from these decades too late, I offer my humblest apologies for the way in which I informed you of your son's death. In my dark hours, I return still in thought and wish I could have another chance. For whatever forlorn comfort it might give, I learned a lesson I have never forgotten. A cold voice on a telephone is no substitute for a human presence in the face of such grief.

The nature of a practice in an area where visitors comprise a large part of it meant that I faced similar circumstances again, over and over. From that day on, I called a policeman or (if known) a pastor and asked him to deliver the terrible message in person. For passing such a burden on to you who were the lawmen and religious people of your scattered communities, I apologize and hope you understand.

To practitioners of three professions regularly falls the task of informing someone that a loved one will never return home. A policeman, or in a time of war, a soldier at the door. By the mythology of our culture, we anoint a religious leader with some power to break such news and make it less shattering. Ever and always, there is the physician.

A doctor is by the nature of things the person who decides

when life has departed. Death is seldom an event compressed into a moment of time. Organs of the body fail in cascading sequence when death stalks forward. Ordinary citizens know of "brain-dead" injury, informed by newspaper and television. One's nervous system is the ultimately irreplaceable "part." Hearts, kidneys, lungs, bone, even lowly skin can be "salvaged" for the benefit of another person. When can the physician certify death under these constraints? When declare the battle lost?

My experience is that those in society whose work places them at the interface between life and death cope with sudden disaster little better than anyone else. Macabre whimsy in the presence of death, gallows humor, is a defense. Calluses the psyche must form are so easily mistaken for callousness. The physicians I have known best, the lawmen, the pastors, dread bearing news of death, especially when it is unexpected. Look the bewildered new widow in the eye?

"So sorry," is trite and hollow to the policeman's own ear. Spew words like tainted confetti? A colleague tells of an occasion when he simply sat with survivors in a tiny office room for minutes stretching into half an hour. Silently. Without movement or touching. Yet, those with whom he "shared" felt his pain and accepted it as balm.

We notifiers each react according to our own inhibitions. My instincts are to touch quietly, hand to arm, even a hug. Trite as it is, "I'm sorry," when it is sincere, carries more healing than a sermon-full of words.

There is, and can be, no easy way.

DR. RICARD (RIC) PUUMALA, M.D.,
CONTRIBUTED THE NEXT FIVE STORIES

Dr. Ricard (Ric) Puumala, M.D., is a family physician in Cloquet, Minnesota. His is the second in three generations of physicians. His parents, Dr. Reino Puumala, M.D., and Dr. Marie Bepko, M.D., his physician wife, Barbara, and he, formed a truly "Family Practice," sharing professional lives as well as personal. This unique group received, together, in 1972, the prestigious Diehl Award of the University of Minnesota Medical Alumni Association. Dr. Ric is a veteran of forty-five years of rural practice. In 1996, the Minnesota Academy of Family Physicians elected him Family Physician of the Year. He has served as county coroner and as preceptor/ tutor for a series of medical students. He describes himself as a bird watcher, a gatherer of mushrooms, a fisherman and hunter. Let me introduce Dr. Puumala in his own words:

When to Have the Baby

Obstetrics is the most unpredictable part of medicine. How can women unrelated and unknown to each other manage to deliver so nearly at the same time? It was one of those nights in my career.

I delivered a baby about midnight. While that was going on, a multipara . . . doctor talk describing a woman who had had one or more previous babies . . . came into the hospital in active labor. Shortly thereafter, a second such patient joined the party. I delivered one lady, ran to the adjoining delivery room and caught the second, then returned to the first delivery room to cope with the afterbirth, then back to the second lady . . .

Meanwhile, on a gurney rattling in from the emergency room came another woman said to be in labor. Her baby, already arrived, pink and blinking at the bright lights of the obstetrical suite, lay placidly between her legs. I dragged on sterile gloves. A boy, the little guy shook a fist at me, winked, then peed on my arm when I picked him up.

I chided the lad's mother: "That's cutting it close."

She said, "Oh, he was born about eight miles out, but I didn't dare tell my husband for fear he might drive off the road."

Our women are tough, their babies robust. All was well.

Sulo

Beginning in the last two decades of the nineteenth century, iron ore became the economic lifeblood of northern Minnesota. The Cuyuna Range. The mighty Mesabi Range, a mountain of iron one hundred miles long. Iron ore mined must travel east to the steel mills of Ohio and Pennsylvania. The Great Lakes seaway provided the passage; boats up to a fifth of a mile in length were the carriers.

The season for shipping iron ore has always been decided by winter ice in bays of the lakes and in the locks connecting them. Shipping season averaged seven to eight months of the year.

Men loaded the boats from shore; other men rode the ore carriers back and forth. Men who tolerate storms and cold and isolation—men such as Sulo.

Sulo worked on one of the ore freighters from first day of shipping until shut-down in December. A man built up a powerful thirst by then, because a drunk during the season could cost him his job. Finally, the lakes froze and the drinking light was lit.

By Christmas Eve, Sulo was beginning to see frightening things. He came to the emergency room of the hospital in our town for a shot "to make the visions go away."

When Sulo bent over the examination table to receive his injection, I noticed the neck of a whiskey bottle projecting from a pocket of his Eisenhower jacket.

I said, "Sulo, you've come for a shot to help you quit drinking, but you have whiskey in your pocket. That doesn't make sense."

The man's cheeks were rosy, his eyes bright blue. He said, "But Doc, your medicine might not work."

I took the bottle from him and told him he couldn't have it until after New Year's Day. I brought it to my office and stashed it in the safe.

New Years Day happened to be a Sunday. Sulo arrived at the hospital and demanded the return of his whiskey. Hospital personnel, of course, knew nothing about his treasure, so he had to come to the office the next day. He left with the bottle clutched to his chest. I have wondered what those patients in the waiting room expected from me when I sat down to write their prescriptions.

I debated refusing to return his whiskey, but legislating good judgment has always escaped me. Besides, the liquor store was four blocks away; his own bottle merely represented money in the bank.

I next saw Sulo two years later, when I was summoned to his modest home to pronounce him dead. I waded through a forest of empty vodka bottles.

A doctor can be touchy when forced to admit that a patient is more on target than he. Sulo had been right. My medicine did not work.

Is That You, Doc?

Maurie died in Arkansas at the age of ninety-two. I'm not suggesting that the location was responsible. Still, one never knows what that fabled southern hospitality might do to a man. His family had told him eons before that he would "live until he turned nice," an implied guarantee of immortality.

Maurie had been a railroad man. He retired well before his ill-fated journey to the south. He had been a foreman in the shop, performing whatever mysterious activities that implies. Since alcoholism was a job requirement, he did that, too. Whether through irritation over his management style or through jolly good humor, people played tricks on Maurie.

Things like letting him sleep in his chair at work, hours past time to go home. Heck, it didn't even qualify as overtime.

I first met Maurie when he came to the office convinced that he suffered from heart trouble. His pulse was rapid, at the precise rate occasioned by detoxifying alcohol. My evaluation disclosed a rousing case of gastritis. Alcohol does that, too.

For some reason, he and I got along amicably. I learned not to ask too many questions (adaptability is helpful in a broadly-based medical practice), instead told him what to do based on his needs. I ignored what he asked for, usually something illogical, illegal or "ill" producing.

The usual scenario was a phone call at 7 a.m. "Is that you, Doc? My stomach is acting up. I need to go to the hospital." I would put him on a bland diet, keep alcohol out of reach, and after a few days he would be good for several months. We never discussed alcohol. Gradually the spells got further apart, then two years went by.

An early morning call again: "Is that you, Doc?"

I asked, "Where did you find the bottle, Maurie?"

"Well, uh, behind the wood pile in the garage."

That turned out to be the last time he drank.

Eventually Maurie graduated to genuine heart disease: A myocardial infarction, an acute attack due to plugged up coronary arteries. Later, his aorta ballooned out, an aneurism. He had it repaired. Bloody sputum led to a diagnosis of lung cancer. Tobacco and alcohol are such regular companions. Removal of part of one lung resulted in a cure. His luck held.

Maurie owned eighty wooded acres outside of town. Deer, beavers in a pond on the place, even a house weasel to keep the mice down, were Maurie's late-life companions. He became profoundly deaf. He often invited me to hunt on his acreage. I could expect to shout at him, straightening out his medications, curbing a generosity that led him to give away far too many of his belongings.

His wife, Sylvia, gradually slipped into the dim world of dementia. Maurie did a great job of caring for her, kept her clean, fed and medicated. She died eventually after a severe fall.

In the end, Maurie became "nice"—and died. I really miss him. Some mornings I awake with a start, convinced that the phone has rung and that I will pick up the receiver to hear once again, "Is that you, Doc?"

There Must Be an Alternative!

Colon cancer is the second or third most common malignancy to plague humanity. Because it is silent during its early, most curative stages, we doctors all too often discover the disease after it has spread beyond the bowel. It is a very lethal kind of tumor.

Fortunately, access to the large bowel is readily available. Today, colonoscopy is the gold standard in checking for colon cancer. Instruments have been invented that can be threaded the entire length of the large bowel, allowing direct visualization. Polyps, those precursors to cancer, and cancer itself can be located and biopsied to establish a diagnosis. Simple, noninvasive in terms of surgery, and accurate. The result is joy and gratitude among patients and physicians alike!

Wait a bit. Maybe joy overstates a patient's response. There is that "prep," twenty gallons of foul-tasting laxative solution to drink. Okay, maybe not quite twenty gallons. Lots, though. Flavored with some artificial fruit that never grew on a tree.

Put the stuff in the same column as an A-bomb.

Next, "Smilin' Doc GI-Guy" hauls out a fifteen-foot-long tube the size of a plumber's snake and . . . not really fifteen feet? Long enough. I guess you get the picture. Enough to make a patient long for the good old days before colonoscopy was invented. Only problem, a few with long memories recall what a barium enema was like.

Sigh.

A radiologist is a specialist whose role in the panoply of medicine is to read x-rays. An x-ray film is actually the negative. Everything is reversed; black means transparent and white means you can't see through that part. Bone,

78

for instance. It takes getting used to, like recognizing Aunt Tillie from the negative of her photograph. Another thing radiologists do is to perform "contrast studies." There are many kinds of these, but right now we are focused on examination of the large bowel. A barium enema. A huge can-full of liquid barium is pumped into the patient's colon. Why barium? Because it stops x-rays, more of that white-on-the-x-ray-film, you-can't-see-through-it factor. It nicely outlines features inside the bowel in the process.

This sounds benign. Still, where one happens to be, standing (beside the x-ray table), or lying (on the x-ray table), has a lot to do with your perspective.

In our neck of northern Minnesota, there was a fine radiologist by the name of Dr. Al Balmer. He would arrive at our hospital for a morning's work. A series of completely anonymous human bodies, clad in large bibs, enshrouded in white sheets, lay lined up on a fleet of gurneys in the hallway outside the x-ray suite. So often the requested procedure was clearly detailed in the patient's chart, but the reasons for requesting it a blank page or one covered with illegible scrawls. Doctors are notoriously poor scribblers. Dr. Al would again be confronted with the frustration of having no patient history.

As he maneuvered a bucket of milky-white barium mix into place, he would conduct an impromptu interview with the patient. Take the case of Mrs. McElhenny. The lady was in her eighties and had been known to wield a mean cane when aroused.

"Good morning," genial Dr. Al booms.

No response.

"She's kind of deaf," a nurse volunteers.

"What seems to be your problem?" Dr. Al roars.

The lady tightens her lips over store-bought choppers. The nurse turns her onto her side, while he does what a doctor planning a barium enema has to do.

"It helps me to know why we are performing this," Dr. Al explains.

A frown from the lady. Grim.

Barium mixture flows.

"You don't have much to say," the doctor says.

The bucket of barium is now nearly empty, the lady beginning to squirm.

Mrs. McElhenny pipes up, "I'll talk! I'll talk!"

Office Humor

A young matron came into my office for a prenatal exam. She had reached the fourth month of her pregnancy. She pointed to her breasts, enlarged by the hormones of her condition.

"Look, I've finally got something to brag about!"

Elsa was one of those slender ladies whose rib cage reminds one of a xylophone. The nurse had pinned a note to her chart: Breast exam. As is my custom, I still asked her the reason for her visit.

She chirped, "I came to get my fried eggs checked."

I puzzled through her answer—ah.

Later the same day, a second lady with a similar build arrived. Another breast examination. I knew her to have a good sense of humor and asked her if she had come to have her fried eggs checked. She chortled and said, "No, it's for my spaniel ears. They're real handy, roll them up and drop them in."

She was right.

"I've been having a cough," Mrs. Anderson explained. She demonstrated. I asked her to remove her blouse so that I could listen to her chest with my stethoscope. No unusual breath sounds. The straps to her bra were quite wide and I unhooked them so I could better listen. When I had finished, I refastened them for her.

She jerked around and looked up at me. "That's the first time a man ever did that!"

• • •

Special Delivery

Minnesota has a long-standing contract with the gods of weather to provide storms at the most disruptive of times. The custom began long before I was around to object. In truth, we Minnesotans have come to regard a Thanksgiving blizzard as an integral part of festivities. What would Memorial Day be without a tornado warning? Perhaps the most binding clause in our contract, however, is the Tournament Blizzard.

To those of you from less robust parts of the land, and for those for whom the state high school basketball tournament fails to raise a single goose bump, let me explain. March is the magical month. Vagaries of the calendar provide a little wiggle room, a Thursday on the exact date this year's tournament blizzard is scheduled, or one a few days before or later. A moving target, so to speak. Nevertheless, Mr. Blizzard Man keeps his eye on cars streaming toward the Twin Cities. When roads are properly congested, pow! An Alberta Clipper proper for a tournament blizzard roars into the state out of Canada.

The stage is now set for the saga of Oscar and his demise.

The tournament blizzard had just departed for neighboring Wisconsin, anemic by then, having spent so much of its energy on Minnesota.

I was called to the nearby village of Wright.

Neighbors of an old man named Oscar had found him lying in his barn, apparently dead. I had been summoned to make the fact official. Oscar's driveway was a challenging series of snowdrifts, but my four-wheel-drive vehicle chewed through them with ease. Several of Oscar's friends had gathered. They solemnly escorted me to where he lay. Indeed, the old man had milked his last cow. His wife, Lila, reported that he had a history of heart trouble, which seemed verified by the array of medications lined up on his kitchen counter.

Usually a mortician assumes the task of transporting a body. I had serious doubts that a hearse would be able to navigate all that drifted snow, so I decided to bring Oscar back to town myself. His stolid, stoical friends and I maneuvered the old man's body into the back of my car.

Providing solace to survivors is a regular aspect of a country doctor's life. Still, I have yet to discover a painless way to inform a woman that she has abruptly become a widow. We trouped back into the creaky old farmhouse, my commandeered assistants and I. I took a place beside Lila where she sat at the kitchen table, rocking silently on a straight-backed chair, a metronome in tune with disbelief.

"I'm sorry."

Mundane words, mine, threadbare from repetition. Always there is someone left behind. A touch on a shoulder, a brief handhold. Silence shared with a physician whose power to heal has arrived too late. Silence between Oscar's friends, cast from the same mold of sturdy pioneer, men for whom soft words do not come easily. Silence from Oscar's wife, a gray woman with wrinkles and work-callused fingers, now alone, wearing a hand-sewn calico dress and shoes "turned over" from use. In truth, I also felt concern for the men who had helped me carry Oscar, the physical stress. They were long past retirement age themselves.

Lila looked at me finally, sealing off her grief. "Coffee?" We agreed, part of the sharing ritual after unexpected death. I asked about her choice of mortician. She went to a worn chest of drawers and removed an envelope.

She held it out to me. "Oscar's mother died two months ago. Just this morning, he . . . he wrote out the check to pay for her funeral. Would you deliver it for me?"

I did. Not only the post office makes special deliveries.

Don't Ask

More than most citizens, a doctor needs to ask probing questions. I did. Usually.

The portion of external human anatomy on which we sit, that located between tailbone behind and pubic bone in front, between ischial tuberosities from side to side, is known broadly (no pun intended) as the perineum. The mores of society dictate that the area rarely becomes sunburned.

Injuries to the perineum and those organs lurking beneath it are varied: Falling astraddle the frame of a bicycle or a fence; a quarter-of-an-inch wide, seven inch-long sliver of wood, picked up from sliding along a splintery bleacher seat; a severed urethra when a logger lost his footing and landed on the stump of the tree he had just cut down. I once had a patient who was a bronco-buster. Daily pounding had produced in him the worst prostate infection I have ever seen.

Then there was . . . let's call him Josh.

During all my years of teaching interview techniques to medical students, the mantra I adopted was, "If the doctor asks enough open-ended questions, the patient's answers will guide him toward the diagnosis." I found this axiom to be true with comforting regularity. Having elevated it to the status of dogma, I am reminded of one time when my sole question was my standard opening line, "What brings you here tonight?" (Yes, an after-hours call.)

Josh was a man in his thirties. I knew, in that way such information oozes about a small town, that he was a bachelor, something of a loner, that he lived out near the end of the Hardscrabble Road, and that he was nominally a farmer. In Northpine, in 1955, that translated as "hillbilly poor." He habitually bore a vaguely scruffy look, haystack hair, beard always a week or so past encounter with a razor, clothing even further past a date with a washtub. I had not previously seen him as a patient.

After I asked that opening question, he stood without a word, somewhat gingerly, I noted, and loosened his belt. I began the mental process known as Reaching a Diagnosis. He opened his trousers and slid them down. Aha. Hernia? Inflammation of the urethra? A lad with a touch of clap is often taciturn about his circumstances. He exposed normal and unremarkable genitalia. I pulled on rubber gloves, squatted before him, and cocked an eyebrow up at him. Without a word, he pointed at a spot on the very bottom of his anatomy. I palpated.

There was a small, hard bump lying just beneath perineal skin overlying his urethra. More than a bump, I found. It extended as a rod-like structure in the general direction of his bladder. There was no external penetrating wound in the skin. Now, this is a fairly inaccessible part of masculine anatomy. My eyebrows cocked over-time. Josh studied the far wall.

I escorted the man into our x-ray room and snapped a picture. Nestled within his urethra, extending toward the prostate and bladder, was a dense shadow on the film of a type produced by metal. I muttered, "It resembles . . . but how would . . . "

Josh scanned the ceiling.

I said, "If I didn't know better, I'd swear that looks like the, uh . . . "

He glanced over his shoulder at the wall opposite.

"It really must come out of there," I said. "I can send you to Duluth to a urologist."

He shook his head, side to side.

"Or, I can make a little incision and, uh, remove it."

His head bobbed once.

So.

After injecting a dollop of lidocaine anesthetic and making a miniscule incision, I retrieved a Bic pen replacement part. Reconstruction: the filler had, uh, found its way blunt-end-first into the urethra, had disappeared entirely upstream of the opening meatus. Then, the relatively sharper writing end had pierced the fragile urethral wall and hung it up, preventing any return trip.

I inserted an indwelling Foley rubber catheter, on the premise that while it healed the urethra needed a guide as to where it should open and where it should not. I prescribed an antibiotic to discourage infection. Josh dutifully returned after a few days to have the catheter removed.

As he prepared to leave that last time, I remembered my dictum about the importance of a thorough medical history, but somehow . . . I just couldn't. He departed without my asking that all-illuminating question.

I have wondered, though.

Rex Green

A joy of a medical practice is the opportunity to know people so well. After my life career in medicine, a few individuals shine brightly across intervening years, defiant of memory's decay. My friend Rex was one of these.

Ninety can be a variable yardstick of vitality. Twenty years in a grave? A mumbling hulk in a nursing-home bed? Skinny little women reach ninety often enough that such might be considered the norm. Macho masculinity must be a liability, for men achieve it less frequently.

Consider the man Rex Green. He was ninety years old and counting that day.

Rex had been a civil engineer. He first arrived in the North Shore area during the 1950s, at a time when state highway planners were considering a major construction project through land included in the Grand Portage Chippewa Reservation. The existing road, a narrow strip of bumpy Macadam leading northward to Ontario, Canada, wound a sinuous and hilly path through forests, around great rocks bequeathed by some long-melted glacier, across abrupt little streams teeming with brook trout. It became Rex's job to find a route consistent with high-speed travel, no matter what rocky ridge might stand in the way.

At the time, my Ojibwe father-in-law held office as reservation Federal Indian Agent. He and Rex spent many an hour tramping about the "Rez," planning, planning, choosing.

Rex returned to our area after he retired. He lived alone, whether as a widower or a bachelor I cannot recall. He was no more than six feet tall, but a straight back and lean toughness made him seem taller. His face bore ingrained smile lines and his eyes gleamed with that glint we call a twinkle. His skin was etched by a lifetime of exposure to wind and cold and sun. He was cheery without being vacuous, serene without doltishness, confident in that quiet way of someone who knows his priorities.

His passion was fishing the tumultuous streams that drain myriad bogs and lakes atop our county's highlands, before cascading down clefts in the rocky headlands that confine the Big Lake. It was because of this enthusiasm that he appeared at my medical office one summer day.

I greeted my old friend warmly. "What brings you here today?" I asked.

"I'm not sick, Doc. I understand you're the coroner."

Oh, oh.

"I was fishing out along Mistletoe Creek," he said. "Found some bones, pretty sure they're from a person."

"I'll need to call the sheriff."

"Did. He said he'd meet us here when you're free."

I sighed, a requiem for the day's abruptly shattered appointment schedule.

I rode with the sheriff in his unit, he following Rex's beat-up Chevrolet truck. We went for twenty-three miles before turning off onto an old logging trail. It earned designation as a road solely because no trees grew between its ruts. Bounce and swerve, up, sidewise, plop into mud. At a clearing, an old logger's landing, Rex stopped and slid out of his truck. Mistletoe Creek chuckled quietly from twenty feet away.

"Now we have to walk," Rex said.

"How far?" I asked.

"Only a short . . . well, maybe half a mile."

I was glad I had taken time to put on my favorite Red Wing boots.

Half a mile can present itself as a stroll along six or seven city blocks or, depending on one's skill and accuracy with a club, nine holes on a golf course . . . or as a grueling safari, floundering upstream beside a rocky, burbling creek in the wildest portion of our county.

When you see the sport of trout fishing portrayed on TV, you are presented with a broad expanse of gently-rippling water, surrounded either by placid meadows or trees respectfully restrained along regimented banks. A fisherman whips a twenty-foot loop of line out, back, and out again.

An artificial fly lights gracefully on the surface of the stream, where a large trout promptly inhales it. The ballet between man and prey weaves upstream and down before the fish comes to a dip net. A demonstration, nature securely leashed.

Shift gears. Mistletoe Creek ranged in width from six to eight feet. Occasionally it poured through a crack in a ledge of rock, which narrowed it to two or three feet of frantically scurrying water. It rushed past piano-sized boulders or a fallen tree, around a curve chewed into a wall of ancient volcanic basalt, across a brief sandbar, beneath willows and tag alders and cedars in fragrant tangles, all leaning far out over the water, beseechers of sunlight.

On shore we scrambled between upright trees. Others had fallen into random piles like jackstraws from a childhood game, daunting as tiger traps. Scattered about lay ankle-threatening boulders: the size of a soft ball, a bowling ball, lunkers three or four feet across. They resembled pictures I had seen of Mayan ruins, covered densely as they were by the moss of that humid place. Climb, skid, ease past or under a great fallen pine, sprawl when a lurch conspires with gravity.

Northern Minnesota is renowned for its crisp climate—its forty below, macho weather. What most outsiders do not realize is that along about the middle of August we can do hot better than a Finnish sauna. Then, there are the bugs. Mosquitoes are infamous enough that we need not advertise their prowess. Not everyone knows about our other pest, a midge we call a black fly. They breed in rapidly-flowing streams, and swarms of them hover in anticipation of any passing mammal. We *H. sapiens*, bearing as we do such skimpy fur, make mealtime easy for them.

The sheriff and I followed our ninety-year-old guide into this brooding jungle. At the time I was in my mid-forties. I was not a conditioned athlete, unless you accept the track race demanded by a busy practice as a workout. Still . . . And the sheriff was a rugged man a few years older than I, but a local boy who had lived in the area all his life. He was in certifiably robust condition.

We set out to walk Rex's "half mile."

At first I managed to keep up, squirming under or across fallen trees, sliding down mossy banks, wading when the stream bed offered the only passageway. At the ten-mile point—all right, probably a few hundred yards by a dang measuring tape. It's hard to tell when forward progress is as much up and down or round about as forward. I hollered at Rex, out of sight somewhere ahead, suggesting that he take a rest. (In conscience, as a medic, I needed to be concerned about the man. After all, at ninety . . .)

Rex reemerged from the jungle ahead. His eye-rolling grimace told me that I hadn't fooled him. We pressed onward. I was gasping by the third rest stop and, as minor balm to my ego, even our sheriff leaned unobtrusively against a tree. I recall thinking, "These bones had better not turn out to be from a dang dead deer."

The bones were human.

They had nearly disappeared beneath loam and moss; only the top of a calvarium protruded. The officer set to work with a trail shovel, while I sat on a branch of a cooperative cedar tree, dangling my feet inches above the crystal water of that lovely creek. I swatted black flies and considered the philosophical wonder of the man Rex Green, present in this remote spot for the second time in half a day. Twice my age, and in infinitely better shape to confront real nature in her realm.

The sheriff unearthed most of the bones of a complete, adult human skeleton. Many had been gnawed by forest rodents, nature's way, recycled resources. We found no shreds of clothing.

Putting a name on Rex's skeleton proved problematic. The sheriff finally concluded, after searching records from decades before, that the remains were most likely those of a lumberjack who had been in a logging camp six or eight miles away, located on the opposite side of a ridge. The man had been reported missing one wintry night when delirium tremens had caught him up. He had run out into a blizzard and disappeared.

My county is still wild and unforgiving once one leaves its few maintained roads. During my tenure as coroner, there had been a time in the 1960s when a total of seven people had vanished into our woods. Over a period of twenty years, three bodies were eventually discovered, by chance. The remaining four lie somewhere out there, awaiting Rex, or someone like him.

Or, are there others like my friend Rex Green?

A Quiet Day Along Mistletoe Creek and Other Piscatorial Adventures

Perhaps this story could be titled, "A Return to a Minnesota Jungle." This time I had no Rex Green to act as guide.

Poets laud the practice. Presidents have declared it holy. A chap named Walton devised a creed for those entranced by it. During my years in solo practice, I stole away to go fishing every chance I got. I never achieved the status of a great fisherman; often, the fish won our encounter. Peace was the prize. Serenity, to damp down stress and blood pressure. Of the fishing venues available, I most favored working my way along one of the lively streams flowing through my beloved North Shore country. Its fish were never huge, but the strategy involved! Barbless hooks and light tackle evened the contest. A ripple ahead? Does an eddy behind that rock in mid-stream shelter a brookie or rainbow?

My earliest memories of fishing take me back to Pennsylvania, the state of my birth. Those were halcyon days, when my busy father and I eased along some secretive Appalachian stream of limpid water, whose banks were rosy with wild rhododendrons. Can a father leave a better memorial to a son?

The village of Littlefork was a dot on a map of Koochiching County in northern-most Minnesota. I arrived there in 1948. The town barber was a man named Gust. We soon became acquainted in the normal course of events. One day, while he clipped away, I mentioned that I liked to fish for trout. Gust insisted on taking me to his favorite spot. We arrived at a vast bog, something with which the area was remarkably well endowed. Gust pointed out the stream. I confess it, I thought the man had sniffed hair tonic for too long a spell.

The "stream" was fourteen to eighteen inches wide! It trickled through muskeg and clumps of willow brush, as lazy as a hound pup on an August afternoon. Gust steered me in one direction, and he set off in the other. I straddled the . . . I couldn't call it a stream . . . peering down into that murky little ditch. A foot deep? Maybe. Sheesh.

I unlimbered my fly rod. At Gust's insistence, I used garden hackle for bait. I dropped a worm into the mighty torrent, watched it wiggle seductively, and conducted it on a casual swim. I crawled through thickets, squished across muskeg, swatted mosquitoes and black flies.

My line got a bit ahead of me and snagged on a willow branch. I squatted and reached to free it—a flash of color from under the shelf of muskeg, those tugs a hungry fish makes—I flipped a ten-inch brook trout onto the bouncy bog! Be danged.

When Gust and I returned to the car, I proudly held up my trophy. He winced. "Is that all, Doc? I got my limit."

That silly little rill harbored scads of ten- to twelve-inchers! Belatedly, Gust demonstrated the proper technique. "Dangle fourteen inches of line from the tip of your fly rod." Lie flat on your belly. "Don't jiggle the muskeg. They feel it." Inch toward the stream as quietly as Moose Styrene returning home after a prolonged evening at the Power House Bar. "Never let them see you!" While still ten feet away from the water, ease the tip of your fly rod between willow branches, drop the worm into the water, like this . . .

Pow. Gust landed another trout from the very place where I had earlier peered scornfully into its pitiful flow.

My final venture along a trout stream occurred when I was approaching seventy. Cascade River was my favorite and most dependable place to fish. Its greatest width was about fifteen feet. One day I waded slowly down the stream, the only way to fish it, because its banks were a tackle-busting tangle of cedars, willows and alders. A slight rocky ledge ahead, a pool scoured out by current pouring over it . . . I smelled fish. When I drifted my line into the pool, it snagged on an underwater stick. Dang. I eased into the edge of the pool and reached for the line.

Underwater rocks in a trout stream become as slippery as oiled cobbles. Abruptly, my feet went south into deep water. I was wearing chest-high waders. This created an immediate problem. Filled with air, they (and my feet) floated to the surface, while my head and shoulders took their place. I was treated to sight of a trout pool from a fish's point of view. In order to get one's head uppermost again, the waders must fill with water so they can be brought back down. Odd how long that seems to take. I may merely have been short of oxygen for a moment, but I swear I heard a couple of brookies snigger.

I decided that I was no longer safe alone along my beloved river, and settled thereafter for fishing sedately from a boat on a lake. Sigh. Just another of those life crossroads: my final fast-pitch softball game; climbing Mount Rose at Grand Portage merely to see the view; acknowledgement that Bridgeman's butter pecan ice cream and an elevated cholesterol are barely compatible.

On to Mistletoe adventures. This delightful stream had a variety of habitats: rushing rapids, deeper, more sedate flowages, a couple of beaver ponds. Like with most streams in our area, an occasional rocky ledge acted as a natural dam. Over time, water gouged a "spillway," a narrowed place producing a ferocious current.

A comrade and I were fishing the Mistletoe one day. We'll call my friend Jack. I was off in my designated section when I heard him call for help. He stood in the middle of the creek, arms stretched wide like a tight-rope walker ensuring balance. He had been maneuvering to drift a line into a pool below one of those natural spillways. One booted foot skidded, those slippery rocks in a stream, and slid firmly between two solidly planted boulders. The force of the current had jammed him tight, and he could not free himself. To help him out of his predicament, I waded into the stream below him, bracing my feet widely apart, while he used my shoulders to steady himself. He worked his trapped foot and leg out of the hip boot he wore, leaving it in place, while standing precariously on the other foot.

A lesson. When stream fishing, as in the profession of logging, it is hazardous to go it alone!

Despite this germane example, I could not always find a companion on the day I was able to get away to fish. I set out alone one day, headed for Mistletoe Creek. The access road to reach the stretch I planned to fish was swampy in places. Actually, quite a few places. My vehicle at the time was an International Harvester Scout, a perky little cubicle on wheels. I reasoned that its four-wheel drive made me impervious to catastrophe. I set wheel locks and headed across a rather damp-appearing place. Suddenly, all four wheels broke through muskeg into bog that might as well have been bottomless, since powerful wheels spun free in muck, while the car rested on its frame.

I heard the growl of heavy road equipment coming from the county road I had so recently left. I trotted awkwardly in my chest-high waders, arriving in time to hail down a man driving a road grader. A friend, call him Doug, was operating the machine. I explained my plight, and he said, "I'll have you out of there pronto, Doc." He backed that yellow monster down the trail I had followed and hooked a chain onto my Scout. He revved up—and sank to the neighborhood of the grader's axles. Doug grinned wryly and hollered, "My partner"—call him Gilly—"is out there with a D4 Cat. I'll fetch him."

Gilly arrived, hooked another chain onto the grader and the two units roared to life. The giant Cat swerved, groaned, gasped in diesel agony, the mud-splattered grader behind it. My hapless Scout whipped along in third place like a bobber on a fishing line. The procession ground to a halt when it reached a rocky ridge. Gilly took off his cap and scratched hair that must surely have been standing straight up.

"By gar," he said, "for a minute there, I thought my rig was going under, too. Tell ya what, Doc, maybe you'd best walk from now on."

They departed and I crawled into my car to follow them,

after the dangest fishing trip of my life. Wait, I thought, I've come this far. The creek is still whispering in its seductive voice. There's an hour before I absolutely have to leave for home.

I caught half a dozen beauties. Hath a brookie e'er tasted so sweet?

DR. C. PAUL MARTIN, M.D., CONTRIBUTED THE NEXT THREE STORIES

Dr. C. Paul Martin, M.D., is retired from a busy medical practice in the far southwestern part of Minnesota. Boarded in internal medicine as well as family practice, at mid-career he added Dermatology to his repertoire by way of a Bush Fellowship. Skillful, jovial, a man of a thousand interests, he applied zest to medicine. He is a raconteur of the first order, and if you want to catch his attention, ask him about The Baker Street Irregulars. While not a charter member of that distinguished organization, he can lay claim to missionary zeal in spreading appreciation for the redoubtable Sherlock Holmes. May I introduce Dr. Paul Martin, using his words to bring you tales from his own practice:

We Know Ourselves

Skin ulcers caused by varicose veins are those terrible spots elderly patients suffer when the heart's pumping action cannot keep up with the gravity pulling on their legs. These large, irritated patches of broken skin are usually wrapped with snug Ace bandages to both heal and hide the sores. Often, it is a constant battle to keep the wounds healing and their owner comfortable.

I became acquainted with Maurice Mulqueen years ago when varicose veins had produced open sores in his legs. We had had success in treating Maurice's ulcers, and he was free of pain and irritation. Now, his eighty-eight-year-old heart labored to keep him alive, yet he always had a smile for me when I checked his wounds and adjusted medications during bimonthly visits.

An early morning call from the hospital alarmed me when I heard that Maurice had presented himself there with chest pain. He, like many of my patients, never missed an appointment, but rarely called after hours. A brief interview, examination and review of his tests showed what I usually would have considered a mild heart attack. We talked about his need to remain in the hospital and my optimism for a good result.

Maurice disagreed. "This is it," he said. "Keep me comfortable." I was puzzled, since Maurice was usually optimistic, and my medical sense predicted a benign course.

Throughout the day, I checked him frequently and carefully. He received the usual cardiac care, and looked stable. However, about 4 o'clock his blood pressure dropped, his pulse weakened, and his usual ruddiness paled. I said goodbye to him as he entered another life at 5 p.m.

Somehow, Maurice knew and accepted what his doctor did not want to think. We indeed should know ourselves.

Critical Cosmetics

A rural hospital emergency room is often the site of strikingly dissimilar medical conditions. Over the years, I have seen children with mundane sore throats being evaluated alongside catastrophic abdominal injuries. Acumen and experience of physicians and nurses organize order from chaos.

Joe Fielder's injury raised no doubt about his need for urgent action.

January in Minnesota brings temperatures well below zero, along with a need for heat in the house. Joe's family enjoyed the warmth of their fireplace, which assisted an over-stressed gas furnace. One Sunday afternoon, Joe set out to replenish the supply of firewood by cutting up some old oak logs. When he explained the accident, he described the wood as "tough." His chain saw strained and he leaned into it to increase pressure. The saw bucked straight back and hit him in the face. Stunned, he dropped the saw, put his scarf to his face and called for help. His father was working nearby; he brought Joe to the hospital.

My first look at what Joe had accomplished jolted me like an electric current. His forehead and chin were intact, but his nose . . .

Brightly illustrated anatomy books show structures deep within the nasal cavities. Interesting. Sanitized. Joe, in the flesh, offered an identical view. The saw had created two open gates from his nose.

The nearest plastic surgeon was one hundred miles away. Joe wanted me to fix it. When I explained what needed to be done, and my lack of experience in such a venture, he said simply, "Let's do it."

I had repaired lacerations of all kinds, and in all areas of the body. I rolled up figurative sleeves and went to work. I aligned the two sides of his nose, using many small sutures, all the while carrying on a conversation with Joe about his "cut." An hour and a half later, he had one nose—and a big smile.

I removed the stitches a week afterward. Joe got his first good look at his face.

"My nose is better than before, Doc," he smiled. "I'm almost handsome."

Isolation

The image of rural America in the minds of many people is often one of idyllic and bucolic scenes: far meadows, streams and small towns. Everyone knows everyone else and friendliness abounds. Strife, grief, sadness and conflict are unwelcome visitors. Yet rural life has its quiet despairs.

One of my additional duties in Armstrong and Godfrey County was that of county coroner. This legal duty usually led me to sites of acute or chronic sorrow. A visit to rural Armstrong one fall day defined the atmosphere of death and isolation I often encountered.

I never knew Charlie Christopher as a patient. He and his two friends, Tom Prosper and Moral St. Claire, were retired farmhands who "hired out" at harvest time. Most of the time, they would appear at local restaurants, uniformly dressed in faded blue bib coveralls and seed-corn caps, bachelors all.

The sheriff called me on the Wednesday before

Thanksgiving. Tom and Moral had breathlessly reported finding Charlie under his bed and that he was blue and cold. Off I went to Charlie's home to ensure that his demise was unaided and from natural causes.

A small, faded, prairie farmhouse had been home for Charlie. When I entered, I was struck with the stillness and isolation of the house. Remarkable for its plainness, the front room housed a large oil-burning stove, only gently warm, and a threadbare couch. Just one picture interrupted the monotony of the walls, a tinted aerial view of the house and farm taken during the better times of half a century before. An ancient cooking stove, long unused, filled a corner of the grimy kitchen. No refrigerator or table was present, and a solitary chair faced empty, dusty shelves, long relieved of any burden of food.

Evening light shone through uncurtained windows into a small bedroom. Charlie's body lay on the floor next to his bed, a simple frame containing a naked spring mattress covered with a thin blanket. There was no evidence of foul play. His position and color suggested that coronary heart disease had ended Charlie's life.

And freed him from stark isolation.

• • •

Mort

"My doctor doesn't listen to me!" If we unstop our ears,
we physicians would hear a chorus of similar complaints.
Busy schedules, prodded further by clinic demands for
production—"Turn out more office visits, Doctor!"— make
hurried medical histories too common. I earnestly tried to
listen to what my patient of the moment had to say. In the
case of Mort, I finally "heard" why he had sought me out,
but it makes me wonder how many times I did not take the
time to let patient concerns emerge.

Near the end of my practice years, I spent several stints as a
locum tenens. Translate that as fill-in or temporary supplement
to the staff of some short-handed rural clinic. I met Mort
during the first week of one such assignment.

He was about forty-five. His physique was muscular, if
short, less than five feet eight in height. His hair had thinned,
and grey would soon conquer brown. His gaze shifted, and
I realized that a thin line of sweat dampened his upper lip.
When he spoke, I heard a hitch, almost a tremor. Signs of
tension? Something to keep in mind, with my challenge to
find out why.

A mantra to students I have taught is that a patient is
always apprehensive. I eased into a usual medical history.
Acknowledged symptoms included vague tiredness, what he
called "poor wind," a decrease in stamina. Yes, he had smoked,
although "not lately." Appetite "too good." No pain. No
localizing symptom.

By the conclusion of a medical history, a doctor senses
where concentrated investigation would prove most profitable.
Usually. With Mort, a full history and physical examination
later, no inspiration waved its hand. Time to broaden
parameters. I gently probed his family situation. "The wife's
good to me." Chemical use. "Two beers put me on my ear, so I
mostly leave it alone." Any anxieties? His lips tightened and he

communed somewhere within.

On a day when a bass is in a lazy mood, it will nibble oh, so delicately, barely twitching a bobber.

I sensed a twitch of Mort's bobber. No more, and no firm direction. Back to the basics. Where did he work? A foundry? This was new territory for a northwoods jack-pine savage like me. Explain what happens in a foundry.

Molten metal poured into compacted-sand molds. Heat and fumes and coughing and . . .

Medical school has its purpose, a premise most information-surfeited student doctors come to dispute halfway through year four. At the time, so many lectures seemed designed to massage some faculty person's pet research interest, with no connection to practical use.

A lonely synapse fired in my head. I went in search of my copy of Harrison's Principles of Internal Medicine. It was there, spelled out nicely. I ordered chest x-rays, found the nurse who did preliminary lung-capacity testing. My proud diagnosis survived.

A couple of days later, Mort returned to the office for answers. The bloom fades from a diagnostic triumph when a doctor is faced with explaining the kind of devastation it brings to the patient.

"You have silicosis," I explained. I told him what caused it, those years of inhaling silicon dioxide fumes. How minute particles of silica irritated delicate bronchi and became trapped in lung tissues. How the body tries to wall off what it must regard as a toxin. How fibrosis—scarring—the end result of nature's efforts had become the problem in itself. Scar tissue is stiff and unyielding. How continued exposure to melted sand would make things worse.

"I can sense your uneasiness," I said.

He looked up from studying his fists. "Yeah, Doc. You said it. I'm uneasy for sure."

"I understand. And I'm sorry to give you such bad news."

"That business with my lungs? Hell, Doc, I've known about that for years. Not doctor-know before, just gut-know."

He shrugged. "A man's gotta work. For one like me . . . well. Only, that's not what upsets me."

My bubble of pride over diagnostic acumen popped. Time to court humility.

"Can you explain?" I asked softly.

"I'm tryin' to, but I'm so damned ashamed. It isn't somethin' you go around tellin' just anyone. Not even Doc Jensen (the physician whom I was temporarily replacing.) See, he don't know either. You bein' new, so to speak . . ."

I chose the persuasive power of silence.

Mort wrung callused hands into white-knuckled knots. "Doc, see . . . the truth is, I . . . I was wonderin' if you know what I could do about . . . see, I can't read or write."

DR. JOSEPH CONNOLLY, M.D., CONTRIBUTED THE NEXT TWO STORIES

Dr. Joseph Connolly, M.D., practiced in a suburb of the Twin Cities metro area, first in general practice, then as a family physician when the discipline was established. He subsequently joined the staff of the University of Minnesota Medical School in Minneapolis. For several years he was the associate director of the medical school's Rural Physician Associate Program (R-PAP). He traveled extensively about rural Minnesota, during which time he was my supervisor. He became an associate professor in the Family Practice Department until his retirement. Dr. Joe is my senior—by three months; I don't let him forget. Allow me to introduce my old friend, Dr. Connolly, in his own words:

A Joy of Family Practice

Ray M. was a lad of seventeen when I first met him. It was the early 1950s. I had known his father during my internship, where he underwent treatment for terminal cancer of the lung.

Ray was in severe pain from symptoms of a dislocated inter-vertebral disc. His family was poor, had no health insurance, and hospitalization was not an option. So, I scrounged around, found equipment to apply traction and lugged it to his house. Weeks passed and he recovered without an operation, pain-free.

The family was Lebanese and belonged to an Eastern Orthodox Church. Ray confided to me, a Catholic, that he wanted to become a priest in the Western Catholic Rites. That was initially a dilemma, but after contacting the St. Paul/Minneapolis Bishop, Ray was eventually accepted to study for priesthood in the local seminary instead of going to Lebanon for training.

Years passed and I lost contact with Ray.

Recently, I was assisting at a funeral Mass for an eighty-eight-year-old Lebanese lady. The priest, a bearded sixty-nine-year-old, asked me my name. When I told him, he said, "You were my physician when I had the disc problem at age seventeen!" His problem had not recurred, and he had been a priest in a small Minnesota community for forty-five years.

We were both happy to share our past histories, and I was pleased that he had been able to follow his life goals.

Imagine, this story started out with a house call on a young man I had not previously met. Connectedness across time and generations is a joy of being a family physician.

When You Least Expect It

Dave P. had a Phillips 66 service station a few blocks from my office, and along with other members of his family was a patient of my medical practice. Over a couple of years span I saw Dave in the office for vague complaints of weakness and tiredness. Despite a good diet/calorie intake, he could not hold his weight.

Those were the times when a service station owner pumped gas for his patrons. His was a busy place, so Dave was physically very active. One January, I went for gas and commented to him that he must have been on vacation in a hot climate as his face was so well-tanned. He denied having been away from snowy Minnesota.

It's odd how the calculator that is a human brain does its job. Standing beside Dave, mine put together flashes of insight: tiredness, weakness, loss of weight, and a heavy tan not acquired from the sun.

Does the man have bronze diabetes?

Now it is time for a little doc-talk explanation. Bronze diabetes, better known as Addison's disease, is caused by a deficiency in a person's adrenal glands. Using tests then available, I was later able to confirm the diagnosis. I placed him on appropriate hormone replacement therapy. What a difference! He returned to full vigor and continued to operate his business for many years.

Addison's Disease is rare. Dave's is the only case of it I ever encountered in my practice. All those lectures on "fascinomas" (doc talk for rare and unusual conditions) can sometimes pay off to enhance a patient's life.

A lecture and being at the right place at the right time and . . . call it a dash of Irish luck.

• • •

Down a Dark Tunnel, Spinning

*By the nature of the profession, a family physician treats people
coping with common conditions: Frequently seen illnesses
and injuries. Preventive medicine plays a large part in such
a practice. In a city, a certain amount of patient self-selection
occurs; a woman in labor is unlikely to consult an orthopedic
surgeon. A predictable shift occurs when the family physician
lives more than a hundred miles from any specialist. Things
happen. Anything! Conditions out of the part of a medical
textbook labeled "Rare and Unusual and You May Never See
a Case Like It." When such a patient appears . . .*

Maddy Shipman poured milk into a bowl of corn flakes.
Fat-free milk, tasteless, anemic, but what the doctor had
suggested after a blip in her cholesterol level. Appetite took
a detour at sight of half-submerged, sodden flakes. It was
more than unappealing; she felt a wave of nausea. It subsided
grudgingly when she shoved away the dish.

Hal Shipman glanced across the dinette counter at his
bride of two years. "You all right?"

"Maybe too much birthday party last night." She waved
her hands mockingly. "Twenty-eight. Makes me an old
woman." And maybe today that's not a joke. Oh foof, get a
grip, girl.

Hal turned his wrist to read his watch. "Time fud-jets." His
deliberate mangling of the language. Does a wife ever get really
tired of her husband's little jokes? He laid aside the morning
newspaper, stood and stretched. "Gotta go earn a buck." He
sat beside her on her side of the counter, pulled her against his
shoulder, kissed the top of her head. "Busy day. Wednesday,
stock shipments. See you tonight. Uh, I love you, hon."

She rested her forehead against his shoulder for a moment.
When she straightened, things seemed the slightest bit whirly.
She clutched the counter edge.

"What?" Hal said.

She shook her head impatiently, and the spinning increased. Hal squatted beside her to peer into her face.

"Level," he said.

"Maybe I'm coming down with flu or something. I feel warm, although my temperature . . . isn't ninety-eight supposed to be normal?"

"You checked?"

"It burned a little when I went to the bathroom. Maybe because of what you and I did after the party last night . . . oh Hal, I love you. I'm fine, and you'll be late for work. Scat."

Hal glanced back at her from the doorway into the garage. A wrinkled forehead denied his brief smile.

Maddy gathered dishes and stacked them in the washer. She shivered and goose bumps crawled her arms, as prickly as though covered by an army of red ants. An urge to urinate overtook her so suddenly she ran for the bathroom. What had been a light burning sensation had become a searing pain when she plopped onto the toilet. Should she call Hal at the hardware store, let him know?

Know what? That his tennis-champion bride had become a whining neurotic?

She got out the vacuum cleaner, dragged it into the living room where the party had left its crumbs and splotches. She stumbled when she pulled on the cord that fed it electricity. An outlet. She squinted. Where? She couldn't remember where to . . . plug in the . . .

Shimmering waves of light engulfed her, yellow and forbidding, chased by dark curtains of shadow. She groped toward a chair. Her ears rang the way they had the time she had accidentally taken too many aspirins. Her stomach rebelled and breakfast churned into her throat. She turned to run for the bathroom, spinning, spinning, spinning down a long tunnel into darkness.

Frances was a night owl. The way Mom said, "Night owl!" made it sound bad. Moms! So klutzy sometimes. Fourteen was almost adult in parts of the world. Like in a story she had read in National Geographic about—some country where people all had dark skin. Not that she really wanted to have a kid, yet. Maybe never. Making love sounded gross. Mostly, although sometimes she had odd feelings that made her wonder what it would really be like to . . .

Frances' alarm clock had a snooze button. After listening to music until two in the morning, she usually slept through that stage and into the one where Dad or Mom screeched up the staircase. "Last call! Move your butt! Do I have to drag you out of bed?" Stuff like that.

She stumped downstairs. A little weak; the banister gave welcome support. In the dinette, she hunched over a bowl of cocoa-flavored cereal.

Mom snapped, "Drink your orange juice."

Was going to, 'til she made a scene over it.

Dad kissed the air near Mom's cheek and waved at Frances. "Did you finish your homework?'

"Yeah." As if I could do anything now if I hadn't.

Her brother bumped her chair with his hip when he pushed away from the table.

"Brad!"

"Don't you say a word to me at school today. Who wants a nerdy kid sister embarrassing a guy?"

"Leave her alone," Mom said. After the backdoor slammed behind her brother, Mom asked, "Has your period started this month?"

Frances rolled her eyes and pushed the cereal bowl away. "Mom! I mean, let's not get personal, okay?"

"Mothers get away with things."

Frances' eyes leaked suddenly and a shiver crawled her back. "It's . . . okay. I'm nearly done this month. Do you ever get, like, hot feelings? During that time."

"Cramps, sometimes."

"Yeah, them. Uh, Mom, thanks for, uh, showing me how to use, like, tampons. That way no one at school has to know."

Mom smiled, the kind Frances remembered from those times so long ago when she had allowed herself to snuggle.

Things a nearly adult person didn't do. She stood up, then steadied herself on the edge of the table when things got whirly. Mom's back was turned; she didn't notice.

Frances had biology class the first period. Ugh-time. Cut up things that had once been alive. She stared at a frog lying in formaldehyde-frozen abandon. Her stomach growled loudly enough to hear, and cereal oozed into the back of her throat. A ringing in her ears nearly drowned out the voices of suddenly anxious classmates. Waves of light swept her up, yellow and ominous. It was like one of those special-effect movies, shapes changing.

Abruptly, she knew she had to get to the lavatory, and fast. She slid off her lab stool and ran, spinning, spinning, spinning down a long tunnel into darkness.

I was halfway through the morning's lineup of office patients. A banshee wail from an approaching ambulance penetrated walls of my office, located across the driveway from our small hospital. I winced. As the only physician available, I knew that its summons would be for me.

Curt Benson drove the rig that day. He and Gil Farmer, his partner, wheeled a gurney at wheel-rattling speed along the corridor to our emergency room. I trotted in its wake.

"Who?" I asked.

"Maddy Shipman. Hal found her at home, sprawled on her living room floor. Doc, she's really out of it, and her color— have you ever seen anything like the way she looks?"

No, I haven't, not exactly the same. Maddy's skin is white, blotched with purple-to-dark-blue streaks and stagnant pools of pigment. Cold, sweaty. Pressure on her skin leaves a persistent fingerprint mark devoid of color. Her pulse trips along at one hundred and fifty, and neither value of her blood pressure cracks one hundred. She is in profound shock. From what? There is no bleeding, no evidence of injury.

In a case where time really matters, teamwork makes it happen. Nurses measure pressure, pulse, start intravenous fluids, insert an airway and begin oxygen. Warm a body as cold as though she had been found in a snowbank. Ray, from the lab, draws blood for everything from blood cultures to oxygen levels. I consult with Hal Shipman, white from a different variety of shock.

"I don't even know why I went home to check on her," he says. "Something about the way she talked at breakfast—there she was, corkscrewed in a heap on the floor. Doc, I . . . I thought she was dead!"

A urine sample obtained by catheterization gives the first clue. Microscopic examination reveals myriad white cells and bacteria. A fulminating infection of the urinary tract, bladder, possibly of the kidneys. Now I have a target for investigation and treatment.

A family physician treats illnesses that are frequent and which do not usually require urgent intervention by specialists. Since I am more than one hundred miles from the nearest specialist of any kind, fate periodically hands me a problem case the likes of which I have not seen before. Name her Maddy Shipman. I consult my faithful medical books, telephone an internal medicine consultant in Duluth. This is occurring before air travel is a viable option. An ambulance will require a minimum of two hours to reach the regional hospital. During the time she is trapped in the vehicle, the only resources to cope with some new emergency will be those carried on board. We decide to keep her in our hospital.

What has happened to Maddy is popularly termed Toxic Shock Syndrome. An infection occurs, often in the urinary tract. The organism is a familiar one, one that resides benignly within our bowel, where it is even beneficial. Our immune system has seen it before and kicks into gear when it suddenly becomes invasive. Bacteria are attacked—and in Maddy's case, breakdown products from cell walls of the organism seep into her circulation, where they act as a toxin of the first magnitude. Why Maddy? Why now? Why does a great pine tree fall during a storm, the likes of which it has weathered hundreds of times before?

Essential treatment of Maddy's condition is what doctors

call supportive care. Reversal of shock. Urgent. Intravenous fluids. She is not anemic, so human plasma is substituted for blood to improve blood pressure. Quantities of sterile salt solution, six to seven quarts before the day is finished, including some buffered with bicarbonate because the process has dropped her pH into levels of acidosis. Antibiotics appropriate to the bacteria causing the problem.

A paradox: not sledge-hammer doses of the drug at first, because killed bacteria will release more of the very toxin making her ill. An idea new to therapy at the time, large intravenous doses of a cortisone derivative.

The day wears on. Maddy remains unconscious, but her measurable signs—blood pressure, pulse, temperature, state of hydration—improve. Right about suppertime she opens her eyes to what is for her bewilderment, but for Hal, the hospital staff and me, deep gratitude.

I am in my office one morning a couple of years later. The ambulance keens of some new tragedy. It sounds particularly urgent, so I trot across the parking lot to meet it at the emergency room entrance.

Gil Farmer is giving a girl oxygen through a face mask. "Passed out at school. We couldn't get an IV started, Doc. No veins."

A young girl. Fourteen? No more than fifteen. Cold, clammy skin. Blood pressure nearly unmeasurable. Veins collapsed from shock. Streaks and patches of morbid-looking darkness, capillaries filled with blood no longer circulating freely. Familiar! Toxic shock.

I obtain a urine sample through a catheter while Ray and Jane and Gina from the lab leap into the battery of tests needed. I cut down on a vein, get a large needle into her arm, a lifeline. I check in the lab.

Her urine is clear. No infection there.

Yet, the experience of Maddy two years before points toward a hidden infection. Where?

I sit down with her mother. She talks at high speed,

111

hysteria lurking in the background. From a cascade of words, I pick out a phrase.

"Wait. Did you say she's menstruating?"

A wild-eyed stare, a nod.

"She wasn't wearing a pad."

"No. Tampon."

I charge back to the emergency room, where I perform a pelvic examination. Retrieve a tampon, obviously soaked with old blood—and pus. A slide stained for bacteria shows organisms typical of Staphylococcus aureus. Staph, in popular parlance. Ubiquitous staph grows on every inch of our skin. A menstrual tampon left in too long. A chance infestation with the bug that is such a constant companion. Another pine tree blowing down in a modest breeze.

Staph is a mean bug when it is aroused. I decided that Frances needed the benefit of high-tech antibiotic therapy. After we stabilized her from shock, we sent her by screaming ambulance to Duluth. She recovered.

Two entirely separate organisms, a common response. I was lucky, my two patients blessed. Not everyone survives this rare but fierce syndrome. The enigma remains, why these two? Even, why isn't it more common? WHY?

Viola

Viola was seven years old that night.

To most citizens of our land, cold is such a relative term: dankness on a raw, wet day; any temperature below forty degrees Fahrenheit; a draft on one's back. We in Northpine smile condescendingly when we hear complaints if a thermometer records freezing. We consider thirty below zero to be "nippy," forty below "chilly" and fifty below . . . okay, that's cold.

Seven years, three months and two days old.

I have seen fifty-two below twice during my years "up nord." Axle grease freezes, and wheels of a car will not turn. I lived through a month-long period when the temperature did not get above zero for the entire spell. Snow crunches underfoot, like walking on spilled corn flakes. Ice becomes metallic in character.

Seven years old is such a special age.

Loggers leave diesel motors running during periods of prolonged cold, for they would not start again in the morning. In the early days of my practice, ether was the preferred agent for general anesthesia; preferred by a doctor in some remote location for its dependability and safety, despised by the patient for its horrible odor. Loggers occasionally came to me to buy a few cans of ether. When poured in the fuel tank, it can jump-start a frozen diesel motor.

At seven, a youngster has not yet realized that parents can be fallible, that they cannot protect from everything.

A country doctor in northern Minnesota sees what real cold can do to warm-blooded flesh.

At seven, glimpses of what a child will become shine through!

Severe cold dulls perception and "chilled" begins to feel warm.

So precious is a child to his parents, to her family.

I was in the second year of my practice. The house my

113

wife, Barbara, and I rented had no garage, so my Ford cooled each night to whatever temperature the weather gods dictated.

The telephone beside my bed jangled. I filtered its message through the dregs of sleep. Hospital. Emergency. Urgent.

My car rarely started after the temperature dropped below a negative thirty degrees. I rubbed frost away from our kitchen window to read what the outdoor thermometer recorded. Forty below. The electrical potential of a car battery leached away at such temperatures, and oil in the crankcase was more glue than lubricant. I would have only one chance to start the car before the battery went dead. A prayer . . .

That night in February was the coldest of the young year. Life-sustaining air bit my nose with frigid nippers. Tears froze on the eyelids they were trying to protect. There was no wind, typical of the coldest winter nights. A moon transformed snowscapes and ice into argentine glory.

Mr. Ford coughed, hiccuped, caught. A miracle. My breath had already congealed on the inside of the windshield. I scratched a peek hole free of sudden ice crystals and shifted gears. It was like stirring hardened tar. The car groaned into motion, its frame creaking in the way such coldness causes. Tires were flat on one side, rubber frozen in the position of a car at rest. Thump, thump.

I headed for the hospital, then saw . . .

My way led past the intersection of Pine and Fir streets. The house on one corner was a blazing torch. A dirty-orange puffball of smoke and soaring ashes, lit from below by rumbling flame, writhed above the doomed building. I drove past Ruben, Walt and Fritz, my neighbors who were Northpine's volunteer fire department. Officer Louie Wagenknect waved me urgently toward the hospital. I heard him shout, "Hurry, Doc!"

Three people lay on gurneys in our tiny emergency department. Fred, fifty or so, was a trucker; his burly frame was still smoking from charred clothing, his skin ready to weep bits of itself after the manner of a burn. Next was his wife, Janice. Her grey hair was a singed-chicken-feather frizz, and she guarded one wrist with her other hand in that fierce way one does when a bone has broken.

Fred pointed awkwardly at the person on the third gurney. "Look after Viola, Doc. We got her out. Thank God she's not burned."

Home fires are regular consequences of the kind of cold we have in Northpine. Stealthy flame probes for freedom from confinement. An overheated stovepipe, a cracked chimney flue.

Viola was seven that night.

The girl still wore night clothes. They reeked of smoke, but were not singed. Her skin was unblemished by fire's torture, her hair intact. And her breathing told me that she was doomed.

She had inhaled air at a temperature well above that in any oven set to cook a roast. Delicate bronchi cannot endure such temperatures. Gasping, she was drowning in the wreckage of her lungs.

Dear God, is not a gorgeous child worth suspension of your rules governing nature?

DR. JOHN WATKINS, M.D., CONTRIBUTED THE NEXT TWO STORIES

Dr. John Watkins, M.D., practiced family medicine in the southern Minnesota community of Wells for more than forty years. We had shared the rigors of medical school decades ago, and I had the pleasure of renewing friendship with this fine, gentle man when he served as a preceptor/tutor for students under the university-sponsored training program, the Rural Physician Associate Program (R-PAP). I am happy to introduce Dr. Watkins, using his own words.

The Challenge of Obstetrics

Corrie was a thirty-one-year-old mom who had two daughters at home. I had delivered the second child, and that course and delivery had been very gratifying. This, her third pregnancy, had been equally uneventful. She came to our hospital well into active labor. The mouth of the womb had dilated about one third of that needed for delivery. I checked her from time to time, satisfied with her progress.

Then . . .

Her waters broke. A long loop of umbilical cord prolapsed with the gush of fluid. To an obstetrician, few sights can be more horrifying. I pulled on sterilized gloves and checked quickly. She was still less than half dilated; a long session of labor looked likely before any chance to deliver the baby naturally. I could feel the cord pulsating, meaning that the baby was still receiving life-essential blood, but I knew that each new contraction of its mother's uterus could spell doom to the baby by pinching off the cord. I kept my gloved hand in place, next to the mouth of the womb, and worked a finger on each side of the cord as protection so that pressure from the uterus could not cut off flow of blood to the baby.

I knew that it would take too long to summon a surgeon and anesthetist to our small hospital. I barked orders to our obstetrical nurse to call for the ambulance and to alert neighboring Albert Lea Hospital to prepare for an emergency Caesarian section.

The ambulance arrived. One might say that for a time, baby and I were immutably joined to each other within the mother's birth canal. I sidestepped briskly alongside Corrie on the gurney while she was being moved. We were loaded into the ambulance, my hand still in place the whole way. Cord pulsations remained strong. We covered the twenty miles separating our two towns posthaste. At the Albert Lea Hospital, I danced alongside as before, Corrie, baby and I arriving together at the surgical suite. Time to consider what a comical sight we must have presented came later.

The surgical team was ready, and no time was lost getting anesthesia and prep for operating underway. I could hear the calm, low voices of the operating team, but I was crouching under the sterile drapes and could only picture in my mind what was transpiring on the operating table.

Subdued voices gave way to rather loud words. "John, you'd better get your hand out of there if you don't want to have your fingers cut off!"

What a relief it was for me to be freed from the cramped position of my arm and hand, and to hear the squall of a healthy newborn girl.

I watched that little one grow, witnessed the sporting and school events she participated in, and weekly saw her in Sunday church activities. She is now studying to become a registered nurse. I anticipate that she will be first class.

The Message Heard

Humor and happy conversations so often take place in the delivery room after the baby is born. One particular time followed the delivery of a healthy, full-term infant. In the making of "small talk," as well as to satisfy my own curiosity and verify my recall, I asked the mother, "Katie, how many children do you have at home?"

"Four," she answered.

"And their ages?"

"The oldest is five."

My mind filled with thoughts of running feet, shouts of glee and laughter, sometimes complaints to Mom.

Innocently enough, I said, "You must have quite a boisterous time at your house."

There was a period of thoughtful contemplation before she said, "No, just call me Fertile Myrtle."

• • •

Alex

Stereotypy so faithfully erects barriers to communication, and human empathy is victim. A Scot is painfully frugal, a black youth trouble on the prowl, a Scandinavian unfeeling, an Indian—

Although his surname was French, Alex was Ojibwe to the core. The man was middle-aged when I came to know him. Bright and articulate, he was skillful in one of the construction trades. He lived on an Indian reservation by choice rather than from some decree of hopelessness. He had the distinction of being what was termed a Treaty Indian; as a birthright, he held citizenship in both Canada and the United States. Draw some dividing line through the middle of someone's home and call it an international border? Nonsense! Boundaries had been created by men of European descent who ignored wishes of Native people. As a token of belated appeasement, the two countries allowed Alex and his brethren to cross the border at will.

Alex's family were important people in his community. Leaders. Men and women with ideas and personalities to implement them. Life was good for Alex, except . . .

Except that Alex was chained to a demon. Alcohol transformed him into a version of Stevenson's Mr. Hyde. Fights, riotous behavior, oblivion in a fog of booze.

A country doc attends every calamity a man pulls down on his head. DWIs and accidents, with police-mandated requests for blood-alcohol tests. Cuts to suture, broken fists to mend. Alex and I became involved in our version of a revolving door. When his behavior became extreme enough, family members or legal authorities dragged him into our emergency room, and I would again spend an hour or three coping with his latest medical problems.

Oh, he was contrite, not unusual for major-league binge drinkers. The morning after or a day later, he and I would sit down for "The Talk." It varied little from one episode to the next. After one particularly spectacular drunk, I levered him into a session before the circuit judge, with commitment for treatment the objective. As he later explained to me good-naturedly, "The judge and I sat there discussing the situation. I *volunteered* to go to the regional treatment hospital . . . after he explained what would happen if I didn't."

Over a period of four or five years, Alex and I danced this waltz half a dozen times. He was an apt student of AA dogma, learned the slogans, foxed his way through the "steps" of treatment, became as facile in jargon as the counselors. A gut level understanding of his disease, and what to do about it? Like water sliding off Simonize wax.

Time did its thing. Another night call. Another ride to the treatment center, courtesy of a deputy sheriff. Another round of sparring with exasperated counselors. Another . . .

But, wait!

One of the mysteries of the world of addiction and its treatment is predicting which victim will "get the message," as separate from those who flounder endlessly. Alex finally heard something, found answers within himself. Perhaps, in the jargon of the craft, he "became sick and tired of being sick and tired." He "got a program!" He came home that last time with a clear eye, filled with quiet confidence. He stayed sober. He ceased self-destructive escapades. He dived into training and became himself an effective AA counselor.

I am glad to have known you, Alex. From this distance in time, I salute you.

Cause and Effect

Effect derives from cause, and logic is satisfied. Such a simple aphorism underlies the science of medical diagnosis. Straightforward. Pristine. Comforting. Only . . .

Time in its relentless procession can drift over the tracks leading from a cause to that effect known as illness. Before Pasteur, how would you explain the diseases caused by bacteria? Progress toward understanding cause-and-effect relationships so often leaves a dismal trail of victims en route. Asbestos and mesothelioma, the unique cancer it causes. Tobacco and the swarms of hornets it has spawned. Chemicals used in industry have felled many an unwary worker.

A doctor must be ever on the alert for some factor easy to overlook.

I recall the case of construction worker, Jake Benson. Jake was a Viking by heritage, his build faithful to its pattern. At fifty-five, he retained the sturdiness of someone whose work demanded strength.

He arrived in our emergency room one evening in a state of near cardiovascular collapse. A work-up revealed evidence of a profound septicemia, what is sometimes called blood poisoning. The organism we grew from samples of his blood proved to be Staphylococcus aureus, popularly known as staph. Such bugs are ubiquitous, growing on every inch of a person's skin. Most of the time, our species reaches an uneasy truce with it. This is fortunate, because when staph does waylay its host, it turns out to be one vicious bug to kill. I sent Jake to Duluth for intensive antibacterial treatments not available in Northpine. He survived.

His specialists were left to ponder the source of Jake's nearly fatal infection. During a follow-up visit, I discussed the dilemma with Jake. I noticed that he was picking absent-mindedly at a place on one finger. I donned bifocal magnifiers and held his finger close. A tiny red spot . . .

Hunches are marvelous inventions. I picked the top off a scab the size of a printed period, and extracted a wood sliver about a quarter of an inch long.

"When did you get that, Jake?" I asked.

He grimaced and shrugged. "Hell, Doc, I get suckers bigger'n that all the time. Who knows?"

On a further hunch, I cultured what I had rescued. Ravenous, virulent staph organisms overran the agar plate.

Why that particular sliver, that particular time? Such are the frustrating questions confronting a doctor.

DR. ROBERT NELSON, M.D., CONTRIBUTED THE NEXT STORY

Dr. Robert Nelson, M.D., began his practice in Benson, Minnesota, before moving to his present home in St. Peter, Minnesota. This true story from Dr. Nelson's practice allows you a sense of the man and his patients (as told to Dr. MacDonald):

Swedish Ingenuity

A major imponderable of medical practice is: How to get a patient to follow the prescriptions of his or her physician?

Exercise?

"Been meaning to, Doc."

Diet?

"Good Lord, Doc, you can't be serious, meals that small?"

Certainly a doctor can depend on a patient taking medications as ordered, for does not the perpetual dieter clamor for a magic pill?

Not so fast.

Mrs. J. lost my prescription on her way home and decided it didn't matter that much anyway. Mr. K. decided the drugs were too expensive and tore up his prescription. Miss A. decided that an herb recommended by her neighbor would do as well, while crotchety Old Man J. told anyone who would listen that, "He'd be danged if any young squirt of a doc could tell HIM what to do."

When his patient returns later, no better, even worse, the physician is left to wonder whether the medicine prescribed had lost its punch, or if he needs to try another drug, or whether the patient has developed an allergy to it, or . . .

Adults are difficult enough when it comes to what doctors call patient compliance. Consider, then, the realm of pediatrics. Oh those many years ago, my basic attitude toward news that baby "Whosis" refused the medication I had prescribed could be summed up by, "Mother, who is in charge?" Raising children of my own, and doling out scores of doses to them over the years, effectively disposed of that flight of fancy.

———————————

Dr. Bob is as Swedish as any resident of Stockholm. He practiced in an enclave of fellow Swedes in southern Minnesota. In his broad Scandinavian drawl, he recounts this story:

Mrs. Yontson arrived at his office with her baby, six-month-old little Olga. The lass seemed healthy except for a noticeable pallor. A blood test confirmed his impression, a moderate iron-deficiency anemia, not uncommon when a child has subsisted on condensed-milk formula, a regular practice years ago. The treatment is straightforward, a liquid form of iron by mouth. The only problem is that, because of its taste, the stuff could gag a scavenger who dined on road kills.

Dr. Bob sighed, wrote out the prescription, and asked the baby's mother to return in thirty days to monitor the results.

A month later, little Olga had pinked up and her hemoglobin was well on its way toward normal. Pleased, even if bemused, Dr. Bob said, "I'm glad to see how well she has done. To be honest, I'm a little surprised, given how bad the medicine tastes. How did you get her to take it?"

"It vas simple, Doc-tor, ve yust put it in her cof-fee."

• • •

Mirabel

Every doctor can recall a case causing yesteryear bewilderment and realize that its complications would be coped with today as a matter of course. That kind of nostalgia never grows calluses.

Around Northpine in 1952, wintertime heating often involved a ubiquitous implement known as the barrel stove. The smaller the dwelling, the more likely it was that a rusty old fifty-five-gallon barrel had been equipped with a clanking metal door on one end and an oval stovepipe fitting near the opposite end. Burns from contact with its metal sides were frequent causes for a visit to the doctor's office. Metal heated just short of red-hot cooks skin promptly.

Most such wounds were of the nuisance variety. Sore for a month, a patch of redness like a baboon's behind for another month or two, occasionally a scar as a lifetime badge of courage.

Mirabel was five. At that age, warnings such as, "Stay away from the stove!" fall on ears more attuned to inner diversions. Coordination is still developing. A stumble, an outstretched arm, and a patch of skin on her left forearm was singed. The injured area was 3-by-1½ inches, representing what doctors call a first to superficial second-degree burn. Minor, even though painful.

Mirabel's mother brought her to the emergency department of our tiny hospital on a Sunday afternoon. I heard the commotion as soon as I opened the hospital door. The cries evoked images of monstrous grief. I followed my ears and peered into our emergency room.

Mother clutched Mirabel in a near-strangulation hold, rocking the child back and forth, wailing, sobbing. "She's going to die. Oh God, she's going to die!" Not surprisingly, the little patient cried as fiercely. I separated them enough to examine the girl's arm, then cocked an eyebrow at nurse Edna

Freeman, hovering alongside. Edna widened her eyes.

I convinced Mother to await in the hallway while I laid the youngster on the gurney in our examination room. A little pediatric distraction, and Mirabel subsided to tearful sniffles. I cleansed the wound gently with non-irritating soap and applied a non-adherent antibiotic dressing. I winked at her and rummaged through the box of lollypops we used as bribes for patients of the proper ages and temperaments.

I caught up with Mother in the hallway, where she paced like a caged tiger with claustrophobia. She clutched my shirt front. "She's going to die! I can't bear it. Doctor, do something!"

I had had no intention of doing anything other than sending young Mirabel home with her mother, but I was on the way to changing my mind.

"If it will make you feel better," I said in my best parent-soothing voice, "I can keep her here overnight. I'll need to change her dressings in the morning anyway."

I waded through a stream of continued prophesies of doom, death and destruction, then got Mirabel settled into our only pediatric room.

The night nurse called me at six the next morning. I heard anxiety taut in her voice.

"It's about Mirabel. We can't seem to wake her up."

Those prickles of concern a doctor learns about early in a career crawled my spine. I dressed quickly and trotted next door to the hospital. Mirabel was comatose, unresponsive even to pinching.

I sent the girl to Duluth, one hundred and sixty-five miles away. My usual pediatric consultant . . . call him Dr. Pediatrician . . . was available. He chuckled when I explained what had happened. It was the last time either of us felt levity. Young Mirabel had gone into complete kidney shut down.

Techniques that we today take for granted lay across a horizon not yet imagined. Dialysis to grant a struggling kidney a breather was unavailable. Drugs to combat profound shock, such as steroids, were barely on the drawing board. Caring and wishing and wanting made medicine personal, but when they were inadequate to the task at hand . . .

Mirabel died four days after her arrival in Duluth. Dr. Pediatrician and I conducted a somber "debriefing." What had caused a response so lethal from a burn I might not even have brought to an emergency room? Today we recognize a rare condition known as gram-negative shock, a full-system assault from toxins released by very common bacteria that can be grown from anyone's intestines and skin. Did a few such invade Mirabel's bloodstream? None were discovered in blood cultures taken. Was it possible that some neurogenic, sympathetic response had occurred?

For me, echoing down corridors of time, I still hear her mother's Cassandra-like predictions of disaster and I wonder, how powerful is suggestion when it is truly believed?

DR. ROBERT P. MEYER, M.D., CONTRIBUTED THE NEXT TEN STORIES

Dr. Robert P. Meyer, M.D., Fellow In The American College Of Surgeons, practiced general surgery in Faribault, Minnesota, from 1952 through retirement in 1996, interrupted only by a two-year stint in the U.S. Navy. May I introduce to you my former medical school roommate and longtime friend, using his own words:

A Fitting Memorial

"The Lake" is a modest puddle in the broad pantheon of Minnesota's many bodies of water. Geographers rank it Number 13, 263 out of a total of 14, 644 in a compendium of these, our glorious assets. It had been named for a Civil War general. So far as anyone knows, that dignitary was never aware of the honor. Little survives about the general's military achievements, although he is rumored to have once challenged Abraham Lincoln to a duel. Fortunately for the nation, Honest Abe paid the man no heed.

Included among my patients was a man we'll call Martin. The man lived on a reedy shore of our featured lake. He had spent thousands of hours fishing on it, knew every sand bar, weedbed and fish hideout. He understood The Lake's moods better than he had those of his once-upon-a-time spouse. Martin often claimed that he "thought just like a damn bass," an attribute when stalking such a wily fish.

Time exacts its toll on each of us. Martin lay on his hospital deathbed. He gathered family and friends to his side that final day and announced that he wanted to have his body cremated. He invited all present to bring his ashes to his lakeshore cabin and share a final round of drinks before rowing out to deposit his remains in his favorite fishing hole. His voice was a whisper ebbing on the tides of mortality. "Cast me . . . into my beloved waters . . . so I may spend eternity among my bass."

He folded his hands on his chest, smiled . . . and died.

Unless you fish, you may not understand how major was this concession. No honorable angler discloses the location of a productive fishing hole! Isaac Walton wrote compellingly on the issue: "Death is not to be considered a valid excuse for disclosure." Directions to Martin's favored hole, its coordinates and depth, had been placed in a sealed envelope, located in his cabin. It was to be opened in the presence of all concerned on the fateful day.

Final preparations were made. The mortician released a classy little urn containing Martin's last remnants. Friends and family, fifteen strong, gathered at the cabin.

A cousin somberly raised high a can of Hamm's. "To Martin. A real man."

Murmurs rose, "Hear, hear."

A brother favored Pabst Blue Ribbon. "Never did a man have a better brother."

More, "Hear, hear."

A younger sister recalled, "He was sometimes kind of mean, though. When we were kids. Once he tied my braids back around a tree."

"Hear, hear."

A guy from two lakes west, a friend from high school, offered, "Known old Martin since . . ." The guy from two lakes west favored whiskey, so his tribute droned on for quite a spell.

Fifteen toasts take a while. A single round demands an encore, then a third, and light of day didn't last until the accolades had fizzled out. It came on 11 p.m. and someone remembered that they had not yet carried out Martin's wishes. The classy little urn still sat on the kitchen table, looking a bit accusatory when it caught the light just right.

A wind had awakened. Waves became more than a chop. The entourage trouped outside for a look around; a lantern pushed away darkness no more than a few feet. Fifteen well-toasted lads and lasses glanced from one to the other.

"Dunno," said the guy from two lakes west.

"I get seasick," muttered little sister.

A cousin decided he didn't particularly want to drown.

Back inside Martin's cabin, they formed a circle around the table and its classy little urn.

"Should do somethin'," muttered Joe, Martin's uncle once removed.

What to do? Honor and ill-advised promises.

Thor lived on the same lake, across the bay. "Know what? Danged health department keeps a-claimin' ever't'ing flushed down the dang toilet ends up out thar in the . . . danged . . . lake . . ."

There wasn't room for all fifteen mourners to crowd into the bathroom, it being, after all, nothing more than a converted closet. As many as could stand and still breathe crammed inside. Being closest, Bessie, who was ex-brother-in-law Tom's cousin's second wife's sister, actually tipped the flusher that consigned Martin to eternity.

"Amen."

Sounded like old Luther's voice.

A Signal Honor

To many people, the terms "country doctor" and "house call" bond to each other as surely as do Scottish and frugal. Old Doc Lonsdale was a fine member of the profession, from the generation ahead of mine. He practiced in small-town Minnesota, in the southeastern corner of the state.

It was winter. Automobiles were a noisy and sometimes undependable mode of travel in his era. Doc Lonsdale hewed to the old ways, made his country calls in a sleigh drawn by a team of chestnut horses. They pranced along smartly, a harness bell marking the gait. Driving a team along a deserted country road requires less concentration than does steering a gasoline-powered automobile. It grants time to reflect, to enjoy the scenery, the crisp air. Gems of philosophy incubate. Dusk lurked in the west, but it was still daytime, with light gentle to the eye.

Suddenly . . .

Doc Lonsdale jerked to attention. From high in the sky a searingly bright light appeared. He watched it bear in on him, true as Robin Hood's arrow targeting Nottingham's sheriff. Doc was immobilized like a deer in a spotlight.

A clap, thunder on a cloudless winter afternoon, shattered his hypnosis. The horses reared and bucked, breaking some of their harness leather. The doctor fought their fright and regained control. He blinked, after-glow reddening slowly in his eyes until he could discern his surroundings. What looked like firebox ash lay on the snow about his sleigh. He got out and knelt. Gray, the substance was gritty to the feel.

He dug a specimen bottle out of his travel grip and scraped some of the odd material into it. Upon returning to town, he mailed the vial to the University of Minnesota with an account of his story. In time, he received a reply: Dust from a consumed meteorite.

Dr. Lonsdale claims the distinction of being the first physician in the nation to have sustained a direct hit from an outer-space rock while on a home visit.

And people wonder why we doctors are reluctant to make house calls!

Faith is a Wondrous Thing

Communication. Words. Fundamental tools in a physician's role as healer. Information passes between patient and doctor. Or not, if the words merely confuse. Russian to one speaking English? Kindly physician to terrified child? Doctor steeped in science to a patient convinced that wishful thinking equates with wish fulfilled? Periodically, I stubbed a toe over patient communication. I am not unique!

Call the lady Mrs. Smith. She was typical of so many older patients, her body frayed from a lifetime of hard work. Arthritis of the type known as degenerative joint disease translates as parts wearing out. Aches and stiffness were her lot, where youth had known no constraints. Who among us cheerfully embraces grumbling discomfort and loss of agility? If the diagnosis be the demons of tumor or heart disease, at least it provokes concern from others, a melancholy sort of melodrama. Sympathy ebbs away when complaints due to wear and tear stretch into years.

I had invested time and empathy in my dealings with Mrs. Smith. I explained the pathology, the "wrongness" of her parts. From what lexicon do you find words that can cross the gap between a doctor's training and a patient's life experiences? Honestly explain the limits of medical science? Prescribe those things that reduce discomfort but fail to cure the incurable?

"Why won't you fix it, Doctor?" was her response.

So what do the Mrs. Smiths of our lives do? Joe spent $2,000 for the chance to sit for a few hours in an abandoned uranium mine in Montana. No physical examination or troublesome tests required, but bring cash. Alfie spent more than $5,000 receiving "chelation" treatments in Mexico at a "clinic" where the sole "treatment" for any who entered its doors was the same advertised injection. What do these "treatments" have in common? That they have no power to heal is never broached.

One day Mrs. Smith listened to her radio. The Right Reverend Billy John Healer was speaking. "To be cured, dear friends in radio-land, send ten dollars to my foundation, then put your hand on your radio, right there in your own living room. Feel the power, friends! Pray with me! Free your soul from its bonds to the Devil, do it now, do it. Send your money and I will make you well. Ten dollars is all it takes. Do it!"

Mrs. Smith sent her money and waited for the Right Reverend Billy John Healer's next program. He began speaking while Mrs. Smith dawdled over her morning coffee. She labored out of her kitchen chair. She explained what happened during her next visit to my office.

"His divine message came on, and I started toward the radio, but my knees were stiff and sore. I could see I wasn't going to make it in time. Then, it came to me! I knew the radio and the refrigerator were on the same 110-volt power line, so I put my hands on my refrigerator instead. Doctor, it made me feel so much better." Mild anxiety appeared on her face. "Do you think it will last?"

Long Distance Medicine

During the 1950s and '60s, rural telephone service was often provided via "party lines." From two to as many as eight farm homes would be like extensions of one telephone hookup.

One day I received a call from Charlie.

"You got to help me with these blamed hemorrhoids, Doc."

"I'd be happy to see you at the office to discuss the problem."

"Can't do that, got no money right now. Just tell me what to do."

I grumped silently but said, "What are your symptoms?"

"Piles symptoms, of course."

"Which include?"

"You know."

"Charlie, the signal is getting weaker; I can barely hear you. Maybe someone else is on the line."

"That'd be Susie G. She's got the same dang problem I do, wants to hear what to do about them." There was a determined click in my ear, followed by a choir of sputtering feminine laughter from other phones along the line. Charlie's voice boomed loud again. "Susie's too cheap to come and see you."

Special Nurse

Narcotic pain medications make the post-operative time bearable. Nature in her frugal wisdom frequently assigns more than one function to a given hormone or other bodily secretion. A neurotransmitter is a chemical essential to functioning of the brain. A narcotic imitates these naturally occurring brain secretions, not a surprise if one thinks about it. Effect number one, relief of pain, goes in lock-step with effect number two, suppression of intestinal activity. Television programs are peppered with ads promoting this or that for what is delicately termed Irregularity. I plan to be equally delicate. Up to a point. Information must still be transmitted.

So, post-operative surgical patients always have problems in the realm of Regularity, caused primarily by those blessed, heavenly, thank-God-for-'em pain-relievers. Only, inevitably, they turn off the intestinal peristalsis switch at the same time. (Is that delicate enough?)

Making evening rounds on the surgical floor of our community hospital was an ongoing chore. Registered nurse Mrs. W. regularly accompanied me on those tours. She kept asking things like, "Dr. Bob, may I give Mrs. X an enema?" or, "Is it all right if Mr. Y was to have milk of magnesia?" or, "Might I give Mrs. Z a Fleet enema for her fecal impaction?" (Hard to be delicate there.)

One night I told her, "Mrs. W, you have wide and varied experience. You don't have to ask me about such things; you have complete bowel privileges."

A few days later, nurse W. arrived on duty wearing a new pin beneath her R.N. badge. It read, Mrs. W., C.B.P. When challenged to explain, she smirked, a distinct twinkle in her blue eyes. "Dr. Bob assigned me Complete Bowel Privileges."

See, delicacy gets you only so far.

A Trip to the Hospital

In my part of southern Minnesota, prairie country offers scant shelter from a winter storm. Snow hurtles along the ground on the shoulders of winds recently out in the Dakotas or Canada. Drifts pile up before your eyes and form crusts firm enough that a man can walk on them.

Reinhold decided to use storm-enforced isolation on his

farm to repair a cattle stanchion in the barn. He strained and twisted. A loop of bowel slid into his long-standing groin hernia. He could not reduce the bulge and pain began. He knew his pickup would not make it out of his driveway, buried under two to three feet of shifting snow. He and a son started his John Deere tractor and chugged onto the county road running past his house. Snow deeper than the tractor's axles immobilized it. He floundered painfully back to the house and called me. He explained and I mentally set the clock of urgency to ticking, that enforced by nature when a bowel loses its blood supply.

"Wondered if you could come and get me, Doc," Reinhold said.

I said, "I'd never make it, either."

"Maybe the rupture'll go way."

"Not likely. You need to have an operation, and soon, before the bowel dies."

"Fine, but how am I going to get there?"

How?

"Maybe the sheriff can help you," I said. Phone lines hummed in three-way conversations, and a plan evolved.

Reinhold climbed bare-backed onto his twenty-five-year-old horse, Beau, an honored retiree from those days when such an animal mattered around a farm. He rode him across-country, through fields, tight in the lea of a windbreak, along a fenceline, past his nearest neighbor's house to a rendezvous at two county roads a couple of miles distant. One can only imagine Reinhold's torment.

The deputy sheriff, Jake by name, had managed to plow through drifts in a county rig equipped with heavy chains. He told me later that when old Reinhold loomed out of a cloud of hurrying snow he looked like the famous statue of an exhausted Indian warrior on his last trail, slumped over the reins of his pony.

Jake slapped the old horse on the rump and sent it slogging through snow, back toward the home barn. Reinhold arrived at the hospital in town, riding in Jake's county car. I was waiting in the emergency room. An operation relieved the trapped bowel in time, and I closed the defect for good.

The project begun that snowy day, repairing a cattle stanchion, was finished eight weeks later, and without incident. Course, it was spring by then.

Is there a moral to the story? I choose to call it courage. Pioneer blood still flows through the veins of many a Minnesota prairie farmer.

Alternative Medicine

Science demands controlled studies when some new therapy is put to the test. Caution and skepticism are watchwords. Does result A lead from treatment B or is a dreaded coincidence involved? Then, there is to consider the remarkable effectiveness of what physicians call a placebo effect. A patient's eagerness to please the nice doctor, the mysterious control wielded by psyche over soma, can befuddle the most carefully designed therapeutic test. Lastly, one of the oldest "treatments" known is one a wise physician learns to use: the Elixir of Time. Don't interfere with a body's ability to heal itself!

I had successfully repaired a hernia for . . . call him Amos. In the days following the procedure, Amos gradually blossomed out with a widespread skin rash, itchy and red. Dermatology is one of those areas in medicine where cause and effect can be particularly difficult to unravel. Skin has a limited repertoire of responses to the zillions of insults it sustains. Suppose you were restricted to a vocabulary of ten words only, then asked to discuss a complicated topic. Each word would quickly founder in a welter of ambiguous multiple meanings. Skin responses share a similar limitation.

I tried the usual treatments, which these days means one from a pantheon of cortisone salves. No improvement. So I did what most of us non-dermatologists do, I referred Amos to a specialist, in the Twin Cities.

Amos' rash spread, unfazed. Next, I sent the fellow to a large, rather famous medical clinic in a nearby southern Minnesota city. The rash hung on in defiance of the efforts by those dermatologists as well.

A therapeutic failure can create an effect on the physician as well as the patient. Doctors call it the Back Door Phenomenon, BDP in case you like acronyms. That is, when your latest problem patient's name appears on the day's appointment list, chagrin prods you toward the back door of the clinic.

Weeks later, the BDP afflicted me. One day, I noticed that Amos was on my list of patients. I peered around the door of his examination room. Amos was not scratching. His face was free of blemishes. His arms were merely farmer tan, a hue stopping at mid-biceps where a rolled-up shirtsleeve usually lay.

Curiosity got the better of common sense and I commented, "I'm happy to see that we finally conquered that dermatitis of yours."

"What do you mean 'we,' Doc? Cured it myself. See, I was in the barn one day, itching like from a dose of poison ivy. Then, I spied them, there on the barn floor, fresh and steamy. Horse apples. I cut one in two and rubbed it on every last spot of that rash. A few days later, no more derma-whatchamacallit. That's how come I'm here today, I wanted to show you. Figured you could use the knowledge next time you get a patient with a rash like mine, and maybe you could tip off those high-priced specialists."

A Complication of Surgery

One day Hubert, a man in his thirties, arrived at my office, referred by a doctor from a nearby village. Hubert walked with that gait which, viewed from a distance of one hundred feet, practically broadcasts a diagnosis of appendicitis. He shuffled cautiously, avoiding any motion that might jiggle his abdomen, and his face wore a gaunt expression. I took a medical history: pain beginning around the umbilicus, then shifting into the right lower quadrant, loss of appetite and one episode of vomiting. Tenderness in Hubert's abdomen promised peritoneal irritation, located in the proper place. Laboratory tests supported my diagnostic impression. The fellow had appendicitis.

The sole treatment for the disease is an operation, the earlier the better. I explained what was happening and what I needed to do about it.

"No," Hubert muttered.

"What do you mean, 'No?'" I demanded.

"No operation."

I explained again, from the beginning.

"No."

"But you could die. Without an operation, you will."

"No."

We doctors do not take humbly to having a patient ignore advice. I've been told that when a patient flips off my directives, my face reddens, my hair stands upright and my voice becomes strident. If the issue is one of lifestyle, say a diabetic convinced that cutting out a candy bar once a week will substitute for a diet actually tailored to his needs, it is one thing. For a patient who has an acute and life-about-to-be-terminated problem, who then refuses the procedure that will save him, steam accumulates in the doctor's emotional boiler.

I reacted. Hubert remained sullenly adamant.

Time crept along its appointed rounds. One hour. Two hours. I stomped back into the hospital room where Hubert huddled in bed.

My voice crackled. "This is crazy. I am opposed to watching a man commit suicide." Some new religious dictum? "At least tell me why!"

Pain is a magnificent motivator. Hubert licked dry lips and muttered, "There ain't any other way? No shots or pills?"

"No."

Hubert sighed like a leaky bagpipe, then winced and clutched his abdomen tightly. "You don't know what you're askin', Doc."

"People almost never have to die from appendicitis anymore. There's still time to get it out of there. And I've done the operation hundreds of times."

"Oh, it ain't you. Okay, Doc. Guess I gotta take my chances. It's see, like, I've heard you use this whatyoucall sodium pentothal to go to sleep. Right?"

"To begin anesthesia. Later we shift to another modality."

"I don't care about all that. See, like, I've heard that that stuff is whatyoucall, truth serum."

I cocked an eyebrow. "Guess so, but that's not why we use it."

Truth serum?

The nagging question followed me into the scrub room where I prepared for the operation. The anesthesia went smoothly.

The reason that sodium pentothal is used to induce anesthesia is because its action is so prompt. A patient can be talking, squinting and concerned one moment, but after a syringe-full of the drug is injected smoothly, he or she is blotto in seconds.

The operation went as usual, no complications. I returned to Hubert's room later that afternoon to check on his condition.

Jake was a sheriff's deputy. He sat in a chair beside the door to Hubert's room.

What?

"Hi, Doc," Jake said and stood to shake my hand. "You helped us out here. We've been looking for Hubert."

This time, I said "What?" out loud.

Jake grinned. "Hubie drove the get-away car in last week's bank robbery over in . . . (he named a nearby village). Thing is, he backed up so hard he slammed into a snowbank and left a perfect imprint of his license plate etched in it. Deputy Luke was here at the hospital to see his new kid and by gar, there she sat in the parking lot. Hubie's car."

Small towns can really suck. Ask Hubie.

Miss Coughlin

A doctor who chooses to practice in his home town faces unique situations. If I arrive in a new community as a finished product, my past is mine to acknowledge. But return to one's roots? Can a lad who was a scamp live down his reputation? Will the girl who grew up next door be granted the authority accorded a physician?

I practiced general surgery in the same southern Minnesota town where I grew up. That meant that people from my past sometimes became patients.

Miss Coughlin had been my seventh-grade penmanship teacher. She ran the class with the assurance of a Marine Corps drill sergeant.

One day her regular physician admitted her to the hospital with a diagnosis of small bowel obstruction. I was called in for a consultation. I walked into her hospital room and introduced himself.

She studied me for a moment, then said, "You are Robert. You were in my penmanship class in 1936."

Memory is such an odd thing. An odor will plunge one back fifty years to a day when Grandma was baking sugar cookies. A fleeting glimpse of an everyday situation drags open a dusty file long closed; we call it de'ja` vu. A voice carrying that certain aura of authority snags the child buried deep in each of us. Primal.

Miss Coughlin. Authority's prim certainty. I had to suppress memory's electric jolt. I did those things necessary to establish a full diagnosis before returning to her room. "You have a blockage of the small bowel, a mechanical problem that requires a mechanical solution, an operation to free adhesions. We need to take care of things immediately."

She inspected me for a moment, then said, "I will expect you to do your best work, Robert. Tomorrow morning you may give me a full report."

I said, "Yes, Miss Coughlin."

A ward nurse regularly accompanies the doctor on hospital

visits. The nurse is needed to carry patient charts; to say, "Yes sir," when protocol requires it, to lend pomp to circumstance. Miss Johnson was the nurse tagging after me when we left Miss Coughlin's room. Her face had assumed the shades of a glorious sunset, pink and red. A fist held at her mouth stoppered some emotion other than awe of the doctor.

I need to digress. To those out of the know, let it be said that doctors as a group . . . excuse me, Doctors . . . grow accustomed to the robes of high office. Life and death decisions. "Do as I say, pitiful patient." Subordinates stand at attention, properly, when "The Doctor" enters a hospital nurses' station. I am willing to acknowledge that we surgical brethren are even more exalted than ordinary, peon-type doctors . . . excuse me, Doctors . . . in the sacred hierarchy of physicians. Ask a surgeon. Any surgeon.

There, I've done penance.

I could not avoid noticing Miss Johnson's odd behavior. "What?" I demanded.

Miss Johnson was of a liberated breed of nurses (a widespread problem these days) and she spoke right up. "I would never have believed it if I hadn't seen it with my own eyes. She had you completely brow-beaten!"

I drew myself stiffly erect. Dignified. "No one argues with Miss Coughlin."

And Finally . . .

One of the pioneer doctors in my area of southern Minnesota told this story.

Dr. Pioneer was called out to an isolated farmhouse at 2:00 a.m. The patient was a middle-aged woman, lying in bed in the upper story of a cramped, creaking old building. A twenty-five-watt electric bulb hung from a dangling ceiling outlet above the bed. Pioneer Doc checked her temperature, blood pressure and listened to her heart and lungs, still bemused as to why he had been summoned.

He plopped onto a chair beside the bed and asked, "Maybe you could explain in a little more detail what is bothering you."

The woman pondered for a few moments, then said, "I don't enjoy sex anymore."

• • •

My Second-Most Unfavorite Job
in the Whole World

Into every life, obligations intrude. Some are more odious than others.

At what point a person must give up driving a car is one of those grayest of areas impinging on medicine. Cherished independence hangs on a driver's license, and no authority in society has grabbed onto the cocklebur of setting absolute limits as to physical disability.

During the years of my practice, the state of Minnesota had no official mandate requiring me to certify competence to drive. There was a federal agency, the Interstate Commerce Commission (ICC), which provided restrictions as to who could operate trucks in over-the-road commerce. I have done many such physicals. For Grandpa and Grandma, however, there were few such clearly defined guidelines.

I never relished the role of policeman, but preference did not always protect me from having to function as such. Grandpa begins a slide into the quagmire of senility. Family members realize someone should take away the keys to his car, but who? Aha, get Doc to do it! I would be confronted with a patient angry enough to skin me for a scatter rug.

Sometimes the decision made itself. Jonathan leaps to mind. He was a spry ninety-two-year-old, erect, confident, trim in appearance. He came to the office one day for some minor medical problem. I walked him to the front door, listening to the end of a story, and watched him climb into one of those cars my son calls a tuna boat. He put it into reverse gear, shot backwards across the parking lot, and slammed into my car, caving in its side. I yelped and threw open the office door. Jonathon ratcheted the tuna boat into forward gear, clipped the bumper of Isaac Samuelson's Ford along the way, and peeled rubber en route to the street, all without a backward glance. I found no difficulty in certifying that henceforth the man should ride the senior-citizen bus.

Then there was Felix. His wife's name was Cecelia. She faced the growing frustrations that go with caring for a spouse who is losing thought and awareness to the specter of Alzheimer's disease. She came to me with a request that I prevent his renewing a driver's license. I explained that I had no official sanction to intervene, but advised her to mention his condition to the examiner who would be giving his behind the wheel test in the coming days. She returned a couple of weeks later to report what had happened.

"I went with him to the courthouse," she explained. "The examiner was a young woman wearing some kind of uniform. I didn't have a chance to catch her alone before they took off together, Felix behind the wheel. They were gone for about twenty minutes, while he drove her around town. When they returned, I sidled up to her and asked how he had done.

"She beamed at me, said, 'He performed like a pro, did everything I asked him to smoothly and correctly. He'll be set for another five years.'"

Cecelia said, "A moment's thought, and I understood. When I rode with him and gave him explicit directions, like, 'Turn left here,' or 'Stop for the sign,' he did precisely what he was supposed to. Tell him to drive downtown to the grocery store, though, and he might end up 120 miles away in Duluth."

Cecelia continued. "About then, the officer shook his hand and said, 'It's a gorgeous day, Felix. Why don't you take your wife for a ride along the lake?'

"He blinked at her and said, 'Am I married?'"

Dr. Jack's House Call

I met Dr. "Jack" at an elderhostel. His story provides proof that no matter where we practice, we country docs face similar problems. Let him explain in his own words.

I was newly graduated from the University of Wisconsin, had finished my internship, and chose a small town in the western part of the state in which to set up a practice. In the late 1940s, group practice was an idea whose time was just arriving. I elected to hang out a solo shingle. Making house calls was a given, and I let it be known that I would accommodate such a request.

I had been in my town for about six months when my bedside phone dragged me from sleep one night. "Dr. Jack here," I mumbled into its mouthpiece.

A woman's voice asked, "Do you make house calls?"

"Yes."

"Would you come on out to Axel Bremer's place?"

I stifled a yawn. Partly. "Who is sick?"

"My husband's ailing and we figured someone'd best see him."

"Can you tell me what's wrong?"

"Why no, Doctor, I'm just a farm wife."

"Okay." I sat on the edge of my bed. "How do I find your place?"

"It's easy. Take the highway south for a ways, turn off on some county road, sixty-nine or seventeen, something like that, you understand how it is, when you know the way who pays attention to signs, do you? Go on that whatchamacall road until you come to Fogarty's, then turn right at the next corner and—"

"Whoa," I said. "Where do Fogarty's live?"

"Everyone knows where—he's John, not Bob, that Fogarty. Then you keep on until you reach Hamlin's place and turn—"

I whoa-ed again. "You've left me in the dust."

Exasperation crackled in the earpiece of my phone. "Well, Doctor Hanson never has trouble finding our place!"

"Doctor Hanson!" The other, established physician in town. "Look, Mrs. Bremer, why didn't you call him?"

"Why, Doctor, I wouldn't *dream* of bothering *him* at *this* hour."

Priorities

An isolated country doctor is unacquainted with corporate America. The most prestigious CEO in our county was the genial, silver-haired patriarch in charge of the North Shore's oldest family resort. He was about as pretentious as my favorite house slippers. A person had to go hundreds of miles before bumping into really big Big Business types. Until, by gar, Big Business arrived up nord.

A mining company owned a taconite loading dock and associated power-generating plant on the shores of our Big Lake. I worked on a part-time basis as company doctor for their operation for nearly twenty years. I provided mandated annual and pre-employment physical examinations and cared for the occasional injury. From the beginning, I had insisted that my first loyalty would be to the individual worker who might be my patient. To management's credit, the terms were accepted. I know from discussions with a friend who practiced for another iron mining operation that he had been told bluntly, "You are first and foremost our man. Don't forget it."

One day, I came up with what I considered a bright idea for expanding parameters of the annual physical examination. This was during the era of revelation when medicine had awakened to the idea that blood cholesterol and heart disease might be related. I proposed that I draw blood to test for cholesterol during the annual exam.

Forget it, was the response from management.

I yapped loudly to the folks who considered themselves my bosses. Company headquarters were 150 miles inland at the mine, located along Minnesota's renowned Mesabi Iron Range. My chief partner in crime during those years was lab-technician, x-ray tech, surgical assistant and all-around confidante, Ray Critchley. He and I had worked together night and day, literally, for twenty-five years.

Management summoned Ray and me to a noontime

luncheon at headquarters to discuss the issue.

A man we'll call Dick was the company's personnel director. He wiped any residue of an excellent example of cherry pie from his lips, fixed me with an executive squint, and said, "Doctor, to particulars. You need to understand something. The business of this company is to make money. Anything that cuts into profits will not be adopted."

I strung together a series of explanations aimed at helping 125 men who worked on my end of things—how little it would cost relative to a budget geared to hundreds of millions; how important cholesterol was turning out to be in health circles; how the workers would appreciate it.

Maybe that last comment was the one-ton straw. Personnel director Dick growled, "Doctor! We don't give a damn about those men, or how they feel!"

Message received.

I have lived on the North Shore of Lake Superior for forty-five years. I have seen ore processing and shipping companies come and go. Mergers, name changes and abrupt expansions (some followed shortly by plant closings.) Experience with really big corporate America left me with a conviction that for these titans of commerce, decisions involving hundreds of millions of dollars are made during an afternoon martini break, while an item costing a few hundred dollars sets off a mass gag reflex.

Maybe I'm wrong. Anybody know?

Stopwatch Medicine

We all know the fable of the emperor whose raiment was only in his mind's eye. I fear that medicine is in danger of a similar form of self delusion. For all the triumphs of science, for all the good intentions of planners and physicians, patient satisfaction with the medical establishment is crumbling. When millions of people face financial catastrophe if they become ill, and when those who must correct inequity wrap themselves in garments of denial instead of seriously attempting to fix the problem, I fear for the soul of my beloved craft. Assembly line health care is not the answer to the problem. Is the model of a country doctor, one who cares enough to listen and be available at a cost within reach, impossibly out of date? If I spoke with the thunder of Thor, I would demand better from all of us!

Medicine and "Business," with a capital B, have always formed an uneasy alliance. *Access to decent medical care is a right, not a privilege!* The constant tug-of-war between assuring such for everyone needing it, and the grim realities of having to pay office staff, buy supplies and provide for my family, led me to consider an alternative to a traditional entrepreneurial practice. I had heard of Health Maintenance Organizations, or HMOs. My public grumbling about the rigors of practice reached the ear of Lance, a leader of such a group, whose headquarters were 200 miles away on Minnesota's Mesabi Iron Range. Lance made an airplane trip to visit me in my office. We talked long. A pairing that seemed made in paradise emerged. I sold my equipment to the HMO and signed on as a salaried employee.

A year later, David and Bill, two freshly-minted family physicians, joined me in what had been for decades a solo practice, based in our stunning North Shore village. We had a dream, affordable medical care without the constraints of that capital-B business.

Another year went by. Then . . .

Today was special. Mr. Barker, second in command with the HMO, was in our clinic for the day. Support time. Evaluation of process. "Let's iron out any problems," he said.

Martha V. was my first patient that morning. Her chart was thick, what we doctors call the Sears sign—notes and data from dozens of previous visits. I did not need to review it to predict that her symptoms would be vague, that physical findings would confirm mid-life average health, that trips to the hospital laboratory would be uninformative.

Time nipping at my heels with piranha teeth had been my excuse for previous failure to dig deeper into Martha's living experiences. Time and its companion, a waiting room crammed with impatient patients.

But time was no longer an issue!

I leaned back in my chair, granting her permission to relax from an anxious perch on the edge of hers. I studied her with an eye untainted by a sense of haste. She was lean, with hands cracked by work and winter's cold burns. Humor had left no tracks on her face.

"My stomach hurts," Martha said in a soft drone.

"Can you explain?"

"It kind of knots up, and my bowels don't work right."

I nodded.

"I can't sleep nights, then am so tired all day I can't get my work done."

I moved into new territory. "How are things at home?"

She started, and I was reminded of the response of a cat when it spies unexpected motion. "Home?"

I nodded again.

"There's just Harold and me these days. Sarah's married and . . . what has that to do with why I'm sick all the time?"

"Maybe nothing. Maybe a lot. How do you and Harold settle disagreements?"

"We never disagree."

"Most married people have their little disputes," I said. "How they are settled can have an effect on how a person feels."

"Harold would never stand for any backtalk!"

Aha.

I said, "Pretend I'm invisible, an observer in your home. Let's say you and Harold have had an argument—"

"Doc, I'd never dare!"

"How does not daring feel?"

"Well . . ."

Martha and I talked long past the end of her fifteen-minute appointment. I learned how Harold controlled those around him with alcoholic rages, why her bowel tied itself in knots, why I had never previously been of any help in finding relief for her symptoms. I arranged for a series of follow-up appointments. I could only hope she would muster the courage to keep them.

My schedule for the morning lay in tatters, but my feeling of worth as a physician, as a healer, had received a vitamin shot. I worked rapidly and by noon, I was only half an hour behind with appointments.

After a lunch crammed into fifteen minutes of coffee and part of a sandwich, I pranced into the afternoon lineup of patients. Click, click, responsible HMO doc on time. Then . . .

Honus G. was a businessman and president of the chamber of commerce. And president of the council of his church. And on the school board. His breezy style did not mesh neatly with my more laid-back approach to life. Our relationship consisted of chance meetings, where I traded comments with him on the weather, endured a joke dredged from his inexhaustible trove of sexual innuendoes, and "Have a nice day!" accounted for most of our exchanges.

Honus had come to the office for an insurance physical. Such ranked high on the list of appointments I would cheerfully have avoided. Aside from its assured lack of any interesting diagnostic challenge, such a consultation raises a conundrum. *Who am I working for?* I am sworn to meet my patient's needs, yet now must swear with equal fervor to reveal to a faceless mega-corporation chapters from the life of a person I know.

Honus' was one of those quickie insurance exams, vital signs, blood pressure, a listen with a stethoscope; good, a heart still ticking. We endured the experience, he and I. I signed the form that made him a candidate for another five thousand dollars of profit to his survivors and laid a hand on the doorknob of the exam room.

"Uh, Doc," Honus said.

Oh, oh.

Important lessons maturity have taught me are that a patient is always apprehensive, and that the designated symptom justifying an office visit is sometimes only an excuse, a ticket of entry. A doctor's hand on the doorknob and the patient's coincident "Uh, Doc," so often announce his or her real reason for calling.

I returned to my chair.

Honus flushed and he patted broad cheeks with a handkerchief. "There is one other thing. Look, does everything we talk about have to go on that chart of yours?"

"I use discretion," I said.

"Meaning what?"

(Office helpers are local people. In a town as small as ours, that means Susan at the front desk is related to half the people from the west end of our county, while Joanna, in medical records, was born and raised here in town. Cheryl grew up on the nearby Chippewa Reservation. A slip of the tongue can be unintentional and virtually unrealized.)

I said, "Meaning that I record most of what happens here in the office, but some things remain in my head."

"Doc, see, I've got sort of a problem. Not something a guy likes to discuss." He buried his face in his hands.

I leaned forward, in silence.

"My wife is threatening to . . . to leave me, if I don't . . . God, this is hard!"

"Try puking," I said softly.

"What?"

"Every so often, a wonderful, wise old Chippewa man I knew years ago, set me straight about life and my approach

152

to it. Told me things I needed to hear, forthrightly, without accusation. Puked words."

Honus blinked at me, then nodded. "Okay. See, I can't . . . perform anymore, and my wife says she won't put up with that. I . . . don't know what to do."

"Tell me what happens," I said. I leaned back to listen.

He talked for nearly an hour, and words that had been halting at first became fluent. I learned about his fears and yearnings, learned what personal affirmation he had come to place on the physical act of sex. What he told me was only the beginning of all that he needed to discover, but it was a start. He agreed to let me arrange sessions with counselors from the Human Development Center in Duluth. When he left the office, he turned back from the door.

"Thanks, Doc. I . . ."

Big as he was, his embrace threatened to crack a rib or two. I grabbed a wad of Kleenex that was nearly as large as his.

By now my appointment schedule resembled the last car in a demolition derby. I slogged through the rest of my list of patients, endured their irritation over delays not explained.

I finished seeing patients a little after six o'clock. Mr. Barker waited in the back room that we three doctors used as our joint office. Dr. Bill sat at his desk; he stretched and yawned. Dr. David arrived ten minutes later.

I rubbed my face and worked tense shoulders. The wall clock showed six-thirty-one. I beamed. "We've finished early."

Mr. Barker was not amused. He spread account sheets detailing our day's efforts. David said, "Hope we didn't cause you any headaches."

Barker halted his brisk busying. "I don't *get* headaches, I *give* them."

Bill sat straight, David and I exchanged looks.

"You, Dr. MacDonald. You made a mockery of your schedule. This patient, Martha V. You spent four office-call units on her, threw the whole morning out of whack. You only charged one-and-a-half units, which means that you *gave away* two-and-one-half units. The same thing this afternoon.

153

"Now, you other two. Dr. Bill, this Mr. Benson. I heard him tell the receptionist that he wanted you to look at a mole. You spent twenty minutes. Can you explain?"

Bill's eyes narrowed the way they did when he was chewing a zinger. "He was telling me about a good fishing hole out on Cascade Lake."

"On *our* time? Doctors, we expect you to spend no more than five minutes on a five-minute problem. Productivity!"

Bill's voice twanged. "Mr. Barker, patient-care medicine is very much an art. Five minutes spent talking about a shared passion, such as fishing, *are* five well-spent minutes."

Mr. Barker wiggled his nose and swung around to face me again. "Doctor, this afternoon you used up three and three-quarter units of time on an *insurance* exam! That company will *not* reimburse us for such extravagance. Dr. David. Your first morning patient . . . "

David, Bill and I glanced at each other, then hunkered down like schoolboys in the principal's office.

We have a dream, Dr. David, Dr. Bill and I. Like army recruits still safely drilling on some parade ground, we march toward our bright future. Comprehensive care. Patient needs primary. Business no longer a barrier between physician and patient. Joy reigns in Mudville.

DR. MICHAEL MCCARTHY, M.D., CONTRIBUTED THE NEXT STORY

Doctors are not immune to the medical problems endured by their patients. Dr. Michael McCarthy, M.D., began a career as a family physician in Arlington, Minnesota. Then, he had to face what so many patients must—serious, chronic illness. The progressive physical disabilities caused by multiple sclerosis (MS) forced a change in his plans. He currently works as medical director of New Beginnings Chemical Dependency Treatment Center in Waverly, Minnesota. Let me introduce this courageous young man, using a story from his own practice. In his own words:

The Stache

"Toxic" is admittedly a non-specific medical term, but one I find useful because of the urgency implied in its definition. I take it as meaning that a patient is in need of extensive and prompt therapeutic attention.

The first time I saw Ken in the clinic, he appeared "toxic." His face was drawn and gray, he was drenched in sweat, and he ran a fever of 103½. He complained of a productive cough. On listening with my stethoscope, I heard sounds in his right chest suggestive of infection. A chest x-ray confirmed the presence of pneumonia in the lung's middle section, so I admitted him to the hospital for treatment with intravenous antibiotics.

By his second day of treatment, Ken was improving. He had obviously washed up; his hair and a luxuriant mustache were now perfectly coiffed and a dignified white color. His fever had broken. By his third hospital day, he was alert and talkative, even giving me grief about keeping him in the hospital "against his will." I discharged him the next day.

Ken was grateful for his treatment and rapid improvement. We developed a good doctor-patient relationship, feeling comfortable teasing one another on various topics, usually centering on our heritage. This bantering started when I saw him in the clinic for follow-up of his pneumonia.

"McCarthy, huh?" he said, as if this was the first time he had heard my surname. "Sounds like a good German name." His grin let me know that he was being playful. Ken was Scandinavian, and proud of it.

During subsequent visits, we fell into a pattern, in good spirits, of criticizing each other's lineage. One day, to soften Ken's continual lambasting of my Irish background, I told him that my mom's maiden name had been Nelson, so I was half Norwegian.

Ken said, "Your bad half takes away any good that comes from your mom's side." I acted hurt, but Ken seemed to think I was serious.

At Ken's next clinic visit, he asked me if I would like to join him a couple of weeks later at a Scandinavian lutefisk festival in a neighboring town. I already had plans for that day, but I could tell he didn't believe me when I told him. He snapped, "Okay," and left the office as quickly as possible. I felt guilty about the bitter taste these last two visits had left in my mouth, and I wondered if I would ever see Ken as a patient again.

It took three weeks before I saw Ken's name on my patient schedule, and I breathed a sigh of relief. His appointment wasn't until mid-afternoon, so I had to wait several hours before I could try to rectify any misunderstandings between us.

The day seemed to drag on. Then, an emergency came into the clinic just before the time of his appointment. A patient had suffered multiple lacerations to his arm and hand from a chain saw. He was lucky, the cuts were superficial, and no tendons had been severed. They did, however, require much time to sew them up. I feared that Ken would become tired of waiting and leave before I talked to him.

The clinic nurse intercepted me when I finished.

"Ken's waiting patiently for you."

"Good," I said. She continued watching me, all the while with an "I know something you don't know" grin on her face.

"What?" I demanded.

"Nothing," she said, still wearing that half grin, now with

"I'm not going to tell you" overtones.

What with the long time spent with the previous patient, and with the nurse holding back information, I was perturbed when I entered the room where Ken waited.

Ken sat quietly. He turned toward me . . .

I stopped so suddenly I tripped over my feet, then burst into roars of laughter. Ken looked the same as he always had, except for one big difference. His exuberant white mustache was a brilliant green beacon on his upper lip. He beamed, pointed at the wall calendar, then looked me squarely in the eye. "I wanted to wish my doctor a happy St. Patrick's Day!"

• • •

A Pearl is a Thing of Beauty

Knowledge is a physician's chief therapeutic tool. Medical tomes bulge with information. The Internet opens doors to university libraries for the isolated medic. Experience hones "book learning" and acts as a sieve to filter pertinence from esoterica. Old Doc can be a special repository of such practical pearls of wisdom.

Old Doc Lyons was one of those country physicians who exuded humor and compassion. I never heard anyone say a harsh word about him. He was handsome in the mysterious way that ordinary people achieve comeliness when character lights features from within. He always wore a crisp, clean suit, a white shirt, a perky bow tie—a different one for every day of the month. His closet must have resembled a convention of butterflies.

One day I shared a break from hospital rounds with him. We sat over a cup of coffee in the small shop run by volunteers.

Old Doc Lyons had a reputation for predicting the gender of an unborn baby that bemused his colleagues and delighted his patients. This was decades before the advent of fancy technologies like ultrasound or amniocentesis. He regarded me with a twinkle when I asked him his secret.

He said, "Along about the time I first hear a heart tone from the baby, I make a production of telling Mama the sex of her tiny infant. To nail it down, I say, 'I'm going to write it in the record so you can keep me honest.' Time passes, baby arrives, and what do you know, it's a boy!"

"'But Doc,' says new Mama, 'you told me it was a girl.' I look puzzled, then haul out my records to show her. 'Nope, says here it will be a boy.' And there it is, written months before. 'You must have forgotten,' I say. 'Easy to do, in all the excitement.'"

It was my turn to say, "But . . . "

He tapped me on the arm. "I write down the opposite of

what I tell Mama. If I have said girl and it is, who asks to see the record? If I'm wrong, I can 'prove' my prediction, in writing."

Old Doc Lyons tapped my arm again. "Here's another pearl for you, young fellow. I have an absolutely infallible way of telling when a woman is carrying twins." This again was before the days of ultrasound, when surprise twins were not unheard of. "Give up?" he chuckled. "Count them as they're born."

Old Doc Lyons grinned at me like the first kid awake on Easter Sunday. "We live and work in wondrous times," he said. "Our ability to do abdominal surgery has been around for only about one-hundred-fifty years. Measure that against all the other times of mankind. Before, do you know how many people died of appendicitis alone?"

A trick question? How would anyone know?

"How many?"

"One-hundred percent of those unfortunate enough to contract the disease."

I knew it was a trap! But hey, he grinned again, a Michelangelo of good humor. It was worth being a straight man. Then, his expressive face sagged into lines of melancholy.

"There is one fight I gave up years ago," he said.

He cocked an eyebrow; I obliged and asked.

"That being?"

"How to protect people from their own folly."

The grin was absent when he climbed to his feet. He waved from the doorway of the coffee shop.

He let me pay for the coffee. Maybe that was what he intended all along.

A New Sideline

*That the human brain is a hugely complex blob of tissue is
one of those aphorisms doctors often haul out. These days,
damage to this magnificent organ can be plotted with an
accuracy down to the function of a single cell. I have heard
learned authorities say with conviction that an adult brain
has more functioning cells within it than there are galaxies
in the known universe, and that a single neuron is capable of
storing a memory, by itself. When something happens to such
a vast but intricate entity . . .*

Elias managed the local propane company. In a place
more than one hundred miles from the nearest natural-gas
pipeline, his was a vital service. Folks seem as prone to run
out of propane on a Sunday afternoon during a Vikings
football game, or at midnight on Christmas Eve, as they are
to realize belatedly that Junior's fever and cough might need
attention. Elias and I have compared notes, sort of a piss and
moan contest. We were pretty close to even in this matter of
annoying "emergency" calls.

Elias was more than a prosaic delivery man. He sold home
appliances and was skillful at keeping them in repair. When my
wife, Barbara, and I built our new house on the shore of our
favorite lake, Elias supplied the drier and washing machine.

Elias' heart attack gave no warning. Tugging on the hose
of his propane truck one moment, he dropped to his knees the
next. Experts agree that a full-blown myocardial infarction,
a plugged coronary artery shutting off vital blood to parts
of the heart itself, is one of the most painful experiences the
nervous system can record. I arrived in the hospital emergency
room, where Elias lay on the ambulance gurney. He was
white as the snow into which he had fallen, drenched with the
sweat provoked by shock. He moaned softly, muttered to me,
"Hurts, Doc." Scandinavian understatement.

Treatment available at the time of Elias' attack included

oxygen, morphine for pain, intravenous fluids, as much to keep open a vein as a need for fluid replacement. When carefully injected intravenously, the local anesthetic drug lidocaine (Novocaine) had been found to reduce alarming heart rhythm disturbances provoked by damaged cardiac muscle. Adrenaline-like drugs provided a boost to flagging blood pressure.

Elias weathered those grim first few days and settled into a smooth recovery. We all breathed sighs of relief.

But . . .

A consequence of medical progress is that every doctor collects a nightmare file of cases in whom today's knowledge would have spared yesterday's catastrophe. Science and life and good intentions are never retroactive.

What we failed to recognize in the days when Elias had his attack was that if the inner lining of the heart chamber had been damaged, nature regarded it as a place needing a "patch." Platelets adhered, blood began to clot in the area affected. Silently, with no warnings then understood.

Until . . .

Elias was nearly ready to return home when it happened. The clots that had fastened themselves to the wall of his left pumping chamber broke free, slid randomly through blood vessels, and ended up going to his brain.

Elias had a stroke, or perhaps a swarm of small ones.

Today the initial problem can be identified and prevented by a juggling act involving anticoagulant drugs.

Elias could no longer run his business. He recovered gradually, remained more philosophical, even cheerful, than I felt myself. Brain scans were unheard of back then, so assessment of which function had vanished showed where damage had occurred. His disabilities were varied and as capricious as though one had thrown darts at a map of his brain. He knew everyone, he had no paralysis, he could care for himself without unusual assistance. Freed from the constraints of commerce, he chose to visit old friends each day at the downtown coffee shop, a few short blocks from his home. Watching him interact, it was not obvious that he had sustained injury—until he was ready to return home. He could not dependably recall the familiar route leading to his house and had to be escorted.

One day the clothes dryer we had purchased from Elias developed some malady and quit. Elias had been the only repair person in town, and no one had filled his shoes. Not knowing what else to do, I called Elias and spun him our tale of woe, asked if he knew of anyone who could fix the machine.

"Come and get me, Doc, and I'll see what I can do."

Feeling like Simon Legree for imposing on him, I went to Elias's home and picked him up. He brought an assortment of parts and tools.

We confronted the balky dryer and Elias turned his back to it. "The way this is going to work, Doc, you take things apart and tell me what you find. Then, I'll tell you what to do."

"But, you don't want to see it?" I sputtered.

"Soon as I look at something I've known all my life, I can't figure it out, but as long as I don't see it, I'm okay in my head."

I odid as he told me. He identified the problem sight unseen, and when I put everything back together, the drier worked the way it was meant to.

He grinned at me. "Don't get any ideas, Doc. Don't reckon we should go into business together."

We had a brief debate before he would let me pay him.

Dr. Michael Debevec, M.D., is a family physician with a special interest and training in sports medicine. Although he lives in Grand Marais, Minnesota, he works in the emergency room of the hospital in the Minnesota community of Sandstone. Dr. Mike's first story relates a "house call." It well illuminates his personality and perhaps, more broadly, the ethos that makes a country doc storied. Let me introduce you to Dr. Mike DeBevec in his own words:

A Date at the Cemetery

"There's the cemetery, Linnea," I said, "and now I'm turning around."

Linnea hesitated a moment, and although she was nearly blind now, she gazed in the right direction, apparently searching for a familiar landmark. "You'll see a little two-rut road leading past an old apple tree. Maybe a quarter of a mile up," she said with a lilting Norwegian accent, the final few syllables up and down and up.

I trusted her memory, and spotted the roadbed, now grown over with alder and red osier dogwood.

"I'll have to reconnoiter, Linnea. Just stay here," I said. I headed straight into the brush where Linnea had directed me, but couldn't see an apple tree near the road. Within one hundred feet, I spotted an outbuilding. Painted dark red, it stood in stark contrast to June's vivid green pervading the forest. Peering to my left, I broke into a big smile and laughed aloud when I spied a rotten, medium-sized, leafless tree thirty feet from the barn. "The apple tree," I sighed, as if it were I who had once lived there. Just up a little hill, overlooking the tree and the barn, was an obvious foundation, probably of the house that Linnea's father had built. As I entered the side door of the little barn, I could almost hear the voices of small children, ghosts from Linnea's childhood. There was a certain peace in that old barn, like that of a country graveyard.

When I returned to the car, Linnea still waited patiently in the front seat, looking out the window as if she could still see her dad and hear her mother calling.

"It's all there, Linnea. The barn, the apple tree, foundations of the house—just like you described."

Ten years had passed since I first saw Linnea Sundholm as a patient. Back then, her husband Hjalmer had decided he didn't like the health care at the New Linden Clinic. Since we operated a satellite office within a few miles of their rural home, Hjalmer agreed to let his wife "do her doctoring" there. Linnea was eighty-three, losing her sight, but mentally sharp. Hjalmer was a semi-retired commercial fisherman—at the age of eighty-five!—still picking gill nets on Lake Superior from time to time.

For the first few years I took care of her, I would just see her for periodic checkups and to refill her blood pressure medication. We chatted about her colorful past as a wife, mother, and in years long gone, as a public health nurse and midwife. She was open and direct. I loved her stories, due to my interest in the history of the area. We both looked forward to our visits.

Eventually, it became too difficult for Hjalmer and her to get to the clinic, so I offered to make home visits. It was a privilege to see her in her own setting. A cup of coffee and a homemade treat were routine. She gave me lefsa for Christmas, along with secrets on how to make it.

I continued the home visits for a few years. She had to be hospitalized once or twice. Her heart. Sight and legs were failing, but her spirit and mind remained vibrant.

Inevitably, the time came when Hjalmer could no longer provide for her basic needs. He pleaded with me not to put her in the New Linden Nursing Home. There was really no alternative, but dealing with his grief and impending loneliness was wrenching.

On the day when Hjalmer capitulated to reality, he made

the forty-mile drive from his home to the nursing facility. He first had to meet with the social worker and business-office people. While sitting in the waiting room, he slumped over, dead. Although ninety years old, he had had no active, significant medical problems. Can a man truly die of a broken heart? We decided that the answer was yes.

After a time spent in our local facility, Linnea's remaining family took her to a nursing home ninety miles away. I could no longer provide her medical care, but I was able to visit her within a few weeks of placement. She looked more pale, tired, and had lost some of her mental acuity. Still, she knew me and we talked about her family. She asked if I could be her doctor in her present nursing home, even though she knew the answer. I politely explained, knowing we were obeying the rules of understatement required for Norwegian expression of grief.

The next time I stopped to see her, she responded to her name but did not know me and was unable to converse. She died a few weeks later.

I still think of her often, even though it has been fifteen years since her death. I glance toward the cemetery on the little hill just outside New Linden each time I drive by, and realize that I have not been to her gravesite. Why? Maybe goodbyes are best said in the spirit.

It had been a month or so after Linnea had entered the New Linden Nursing Home that I had showed up on my day off to take her the twenty-five miles to her original family homestead. It had been a day to tell stories, to see and hear each other. My eyes, her mind. It had been my final gift to her.

Or, was it her final gift to me?

Black Rock Baby

"Contraction!" she said.

"Deep breath," I said. "Hold it. Push! Push, push, push."

There had not been much movement of the baby's head down the birth canal during the past hour. It was still quite high in its mother's pelvis. I felt a "caput" forming, a swelling of the baby's scalp over the presenting part of its head as it tried unsuccessfully to squeeze through the birth passage.

Barb and Tim Griffin had two children already and were veterans of the labor experience. Both had the benefit of easy-going, friendly personalities and, luckily for me, neither was prone to anxiety. We had talked easily and freely throughout early labor, which for Barb was typically short, no more than three hours. At present she was already dilated six centimeters (doctor talk meaning that the mouth of her womb had opened by a bit more than half). I knew that things could go rapidly. Or, maybe not.

Father-to-be Tim was in the labor room. "Take a deep breath in. Blow it all out and relax," I said to Barb at the conclusion of the contraction.

The clock told its story. Barb had been in labor for three hours since she had entered the hospital door. The mouth of her womb was now fully opened up. I had been able to detect that the position of the baby's head was posterior, not anterior, nature's favored position, meaning face up, not face down. Meaning that the head has difficulty completing its journey through the birth passage if things continued in the same way. Barb was a tall, big-boned woman—one that an unsuspicious practitioner would assume would allow an easy birth. I now knew different.

I glanced at Tim Griffin. I knew that he read my eyes accurately. Barb, working so hard, concentrating so hard, remained oblivious.

It was time to explain. "Barb, the head is posterior, not low enough to use forceps to turn the baby. Folks, we'll have to head for Duluth." One-hundred-twenty miles away.

I told the nurses to call the ambulance crew and gave orders for equipment needed to go along.

I had delivered a few hundred babies by this time in my career, half of them in small rural hospitals, half in a large hospital during residency training. I had been in New Linden for eight years and knew the joys and perils of a remote, full-service family practice. A potential hazard is resuscitating a baby after a difficult labor.

The transfer time from our hospital to one in Duluth was 1½-2 hours. I had made that trip half a dozen times with women in labor; in each case a healthy baby had been born in Duluth. Still, that is a long trip for a woman in pain and a baby that needed to squeeze out of a tight place and get some air.

Barb continued to have good-quality contractions. She lay patiently on the ambulance cart, strapped down for safety, awaiting loading.

A nurse handed me the baby resuscitation equipment I had requested. "Let's get going," I said to the emergency medical technicians (EMTs). I could see that Barb was concerned, knowing that she had to endure at least two more hours of periodic pain.

We slammed the rear door of the ambulance shut, turned on flashing red lights, and left the back door of the hospital. Riding in the ambulance over the next half hour, I reviewed the possibilities. Posterior presentations—when the baby comes through the birth canal face up—can result in two outcomes. No, three, I thought. The baby could stop where it is, requiring surgical intervention; complete birth in its face-up position, no matter the difficulty; or rotate one-hundred-eighty degrees and deliver the usual way, face down. In the last case, labor often then proceeds rapidly and the baby gets its wish. Fine, but the baby might be in distress by that time. *Thoughts to comfort a doctor riding in a wailing ambulance, racing through darkness.*

We reached Black Rock Bay, forty miles from New Linden on the highway to Duluth. Besides a beautiful view of Big Lake sunsets, there is not much there, save a railroad overpass. It was pitch dark by the time we reached this place, red lights puncturing the darkness, the speedometer needle steady at seventy miles an hour. There is a wide gravel shoulder.

Barb had become more agitated and her contractions had speeded up, become more intense. I rechecked the position of the baby's head.

"Pull over, boys," I called to the EMTs, "we're going

to have a baby." I kept my voice matter-of-fact, belying my gut, which was anticipating all the "worsts" detailed in an obstetrical textbook. I said to Barb, "The baby is rotating, which means its head will be crowning shortly."

She knew what crowning meant, that first glimpse of baby hair at the vaginal opening. The infant's heart tones were audible and strong. Barb still had the strength to cooperate with my coaching through her contractions. Once the head finished rotating, the baby came right down and was born. I remember a welcome and amazing calm as I caught the baby. Although light was not the best there in the back of the ambulance, the baby breathed, pinked up and showed vigorous activity right away. I gently suctioned its mouth and nostrils. I placed the baby on Barb's abdomen and announced, "It's a boy." I confess to breathing a sigh of relief myself.

"Well, boys," I said to the EMT crew, "let's turn around and go home."

So far as anyone could remember, Baby Boy Griffin was the only child ever born at Black Rock Bay, and he was the only one I ever delivered in an ambulance. I'm not sure what his parents acknowledged for his birth certificate as "Place of Birth."

• • •

Jan Torkelson

My north country is home to a bewitching variety of people. Descendents of gnarled pioneers, those sturdy lumbermen and fishermen, live comfortably alongside newcomers . . . defined as any who have arrived within the past fifty years . . . and lifestyles meld like peas from the same patch. To survive "up nord" requires ingenuity, flexibility, and a willingness to work, even at tasks outside one's formal training. Let me show the way.

Garrison Keillor, of "A Prairie Home Companion" acclaim, enjoys a popularity spanning the country. I'm not certain that some of my California friends realize he is kidding about us Minnesotans. He describes my gender as . . . well, in my case "good looking" sabotages reality. When it comes to northern women, fact and his whimsy mesh. Northwoods women are strong. Jan Torkelson was a daughter of northern Minnesota.

Running a resort may strike some frazzled city dweller as a romantic adventure. Ask those who know! At the time I knew Jan, winter sports, skiing, snowmobiling and romping in the snow had not become the passions they are today. When a year's livelihood must be gleaned during a six-or seven-month period, work and worry rule.

We northwoods folks sometimes term Labor Day "Liberation Day." A time when most visitors have returned home. A time when life again allows a midmorning coffee break. A time when a person can run into town merely to visit a relative or friend. In my practice, I came to identify what I called Resort Owner's Malady—September exhaustion from summer's frantic efforts.

Jan was co-owner of a resort beside one of our county's gorgeous deep-water lakes. She rented canoes and camping equipment as part of her program. She accepted the exigencies of her life—work and hours that knew no boundaries.

She first came to see me one day during the middle of the

summer. Busy time. I'm tired, she explained, can't seem to get enough rest. A kind of weakness. Even her eyes felt tired in some hard-to-describe way. She told how she was used to eighteen-hour days. But now . . .

In Jan's case, I did the things a doctor does before launching into the realm of wear and tear of the psyche. Ruling out physical causes of general weariness can be an exhaustive process. A week later I ushered her back into my office and sat opposite her. Report time. I studied her.

Jan was about thirty-five. Her muscles were lean, not the flamboyant extravagances of a weight lifter. Functional. Her complexion was Scandinavian, with red hair to match. She customarily wore confidence like a robe, an awareness of her own strength that was free of cockiness. Her approach to life was direct. "I tell it like it is, Doc, and I expect you to do the same."

I sighed inside, out of sight. Well and good, the idea of frankness. Still, I have had few patients who cherished a diagnosis of emotional fatigue. Maybe Jan was the exception.

"Busy summer?" I asked.

"Usual. Resort is full next three weeks in a row."

"Getting you down a bit?"

"How can being able to pay the mortgage get you down?"

"Still, things can catch up with a person. Even one as ambitious as you. Any trouble sleeping?"

"No."

"How has all this been for you?"

"Stinks."

That for open-ended questions.

"Any feelings of depression? Life not worth the trouble?"

"I'm depressed because I poop out halfway through the morning."

"How do you and your partner get along?"

"Been friends since college, and Doc, if I'm picking up your drift, you haven't been listening worth moose gems."

Aha, time to really listen.

"Fill me in," I said.

"Told you, halfway through the morning, I get all weak."

"Do you mean that you start out the day okay?"

"Now you're starting to hear."

"Give me an example."

"I carry a canoe down to the lake on my shoulders a dozen times a day. Last few days, I barely got it up at all, then had to stop and rest between the shed and the dock. Twice! Yesterday morning, I dropped a Grumman when I tried to hoist it."

"How, drop?"

"Told you, Doc, I got all weak. Couldn't heft it."

At the time this was occurring, I had been in practice for twenty-five years. Medical school and its pearls-of-wisdom factory was a shadowed memory, details dimming in the twilights of time. Something tickled an obscure gray cell in a remote corner of my brain.

"How far can you walk?" I asked.

"I can hike all day. Could. Now, I don't know."

I stood up. "Are you game to try something?"

"That's why I'm here."

I led her to our small procedure room and dragged out the wooden two-step stile that Clarence, our resident genius of maintenance, had hammered together for use in the then-current form of cardiac stress-testing. Up two steps and down the other side. Pivot and make a return trip, all the while hooked up to an EKG machine.

I left her sitting on a chair while I detoured to our small library. I dragged my copy of Dr. Harrison's *Principles of Internal Medicine* from its resting place and found the page I needed.

I stopped at the nurses' station and filled a syringe with the required medication before returning to the procedure room.

"Would you be able, and willing, to walk up and over our steps for, say, the next eight to ten minutes?"

She cocked an eyebrow but shrugged. "No sweat."

She crossed our small stile once, twice, five times, ten, fif—the look on her face alerted me and I jumped in front of the steps. I caught her under the arms or she would have fallen to her knees!

I eased her onto the examination table, by this time as anxious as she. I filched an antique *Time* magazine from the waiting room and asked her to read aloud. She began an article. After a minute or two her words began to slur. I had her follow my finger as I moved it around before her face. Her eye movements lagged noticeably after a few seconds. She tipped back her head to peer past sagging eyelids.

I stood beside the table. "I'm really listening to you now. Would you let me try one more thing? An intravenous injection of something called Tensilon. Then, after a few minutes, I'll have you climb our staircase again."

She agreed. I gave her the drug.

When I helped her to her feet to begin, she said, "Why, I feel stronger. What was in that shot?"

Jan climbed the stairway forty times before I stopped her, enough to arrive at a diagnosis.

We sat in my consultation room. Her face was smooth, even ironed out, I realized. Another sign.

There is little gained from pussy-footing around when giving difficult news. I told her. Jan had myasthenia gravis. The disease is rare; by any odds, Jan would be the only case of it that I would encounter during my career. It is probably another of those weird autoimmune diseases that keep emerging from hiding, a situation in which one's body decides that a healthy part of itself is enemy and turns the fury of a very effective immune system loose on body systems we hold dear. In this case, its target was the neuromuscular junction points where a muscle receives instructions to contract. Although treatment of a sort existed, it was not a cure.

Jan would not hoist any more canoes onto her shoulders.

So, You Want to Be a Doctor

And finally . . .

Myriad pathways lead to medical school. The funnel-like system ever narrowing a stream of applicants begins when a student attends a quality college. A degree in science helps, although one in the arts or humanities is regarded more favorably than it once was. Medical aptitude tests loom like thunderheads sweeping across southern Minnesota's rolling plains. Unavoidable, terrifying. Perhaps the scion of an intergenerational medical family has a slight edge when it comes to college acceptance.

Stay hopeful, you who are female, who spring from farm, mine, reservation, small town or middle-class city, church-attending or agnostic America. I have known and worked with more of you than I have with those for whom medicine had been preordained.

Medicine has "a thousand mansions." There is one prepared for the generous of heart who sees medicine as a commitment to service. There is one prepared for she who worships pure science, who rarely meets those who benefit from her work. There is one prepared for that pioneer so confident by nature that he does not shy from innovative surgery or treatments just beyond established borders. There is one prepared for the comforter who willingly attends to everyday afflictions. Of the young and very young. Of those at the far end of a life. Another is prepared for he who heals the crumpled psyche.

My doorway leading to medical school opened one afternoon in Iowa's grubby Camp Dodge Army Induction Center. It was the fall of 1942. I was in my second year of college, and a fledgling army recruit. A sergeant sat across his desk from me.

"Ever thought about going to medical school?" he growled.

(I later found out that sergeants regard growling as

173

normal human interaction. Most of them. Congenial, soft-spoken medical-school classmate Sgt. Jerome Keefe was a glowing exception.)

"Medical school?" I said.

"We need doctors in the service. Your aptitude test scores suggest you might make it."

"The, uh, alternative?"

"We also need infantrymen."

"How do I get to be a doctor?"

He shrugged. "It would help if you were accepted by a qualified medical school in the next three months."

Motivation is the spark plug to a life. My father happened to be dean of men in Minnesota's Winona State Teachers College. After weighing the options for nearly ten minutes, I called him. He contacted Dr. Harold Diehl, then dean of the Minnesota Medical School, and I received application blanks within the week. I was accepted.

Where is medicine headed today? I see a forest of paradox. Science and technology burst ahead like the shock wave of an explosion. Yesterday's science fiction is today's power to heal. Yet, people in our country and around the world go without fundamental care. Immunizations. Medicines to abate epidemics. Clean water and adequate sewage disposal! Protection from insects that spread disease. How does the latest life-saving drug provide a cure when it hides on a pharmacist's shelf, sequestered behind the barrier of an unaffordable price? Fewer can afford health insurance at the same time that politicians demand cuts in safety-net programs, this in the name of economy.

Does society worship so compulsively at the altar of money that we can see no way clear to the provision of adequate medical care for all?

Access to appropriate medical care is a right, not a privilege! In the same sense, our society demands, and pays for, other rights that are as fundamental. Safe, potable water from the kitchen tap. Disposal of sewage. Oversight of food supplies. Safety standards for public conveyances. Licensure of health professionals and others where public well-being is at stake. Protectors—firemen, police, military forces—are guaranteed by some unit of government, not left to a patchwork of profit-oriented insurance companies. *I believe mandated universal health care to be a principle decades past its time.* Indeed, more than one path leads to such a goal: a social "security"-like federal program, a patchwork of state programs, some compromise with (and a sufficient degree of control over) the insurance industry.

Does not the very word "insurance" denote certainty? Yet, jousting with one's health insurer for coverage that has been promised is frequent. We Americans claim fealty to justice. If, we may, call it compassion. I submit, *in justice*, that no honest citizen should be faced with having to choose between food and a vital medication. Would that this were the reality!

Sixty years ago, when I was beginning my practice, the bugaboo raised at the idea of universal health care was that it would be socialized medicine. I was still immersed in learning my craft, and political winds wailed in someone else's backyard. I shrugged and echoed colleagues more attuned to politics. Years later, after watching the financial impact of my medical decisions on so many of my patients, I came to realize that the quality and availability of medical care based on the health of one's bank account was wrong. Unjust!

Until a doctor acquires the infallibility of a robot, a computer, he and she will sometimes stumble. A patient may be injured. Doctors are warned by their own organizations and the companies that insure them never to admit a mistake. Common humanity and compassion fall victim to a fear of litigation that drives a physician and his patients apart. Students of law provide the very safeguards that define and ensure civilization. Physicians provide the safeguards against indifferent nature and disease. Are not most practitioners from these two professions honest, caring and compassionate? I accept the premise as a given, then am confounded by our mutual distrust. I have known doctors who refuse to treat attorneys "for fear of being sued." I hear lawyers rail at doctors as being "conniving vultures," interested only in a large income.

I challenge our two noble professions: Is there *truly* no way that a patient can be compensated for *real* injury, in a spirit of humility, trust and respect?

It is said that one can never return home, return to his roots, return to a simpler time of life. Perhaps not. Who would forego the benefits of scientific progress? When I talk to younger doctors these days, I often hear cynicism. Some look toward retirement while they are in the fruitful years of a career, as though the burden looming ahead is overpowering.

I hear discouragement from having to spar with insurance companies over medical issues, from coping with avalanches of paperwork. Some medical decisions seem designed more to protect the doctor from theoretical legal hazards than to meet a patient's needs. *Productivity* is the catchword in many a clinic and HMO.

What did we old country doctors have that I sense is missing today? Long hours of work? True. Alone at times, faced with problems when skilled help would have been so welcome? Oh, yes.

What I understood during those decades in my beloved northwoods was that I was needed, that my neighbors and patients considered me a friend, that life was seldom boring. Anything that can happen to a person can send him or her to the office or emergency room of a country doctor.

Nostalgia can blunt the sharp edges of reality. Still, I choose to believe that we enjoyed special times during those years in the country. Are there candidates to replace us waiting in the wings? Physicians who understand that the very word means healer? Can the rigors of science wed with the compassions of that era, tinted golden by memory?

How about it, young colleagues?

THE END